INCREDIBLE
INVENTIONS

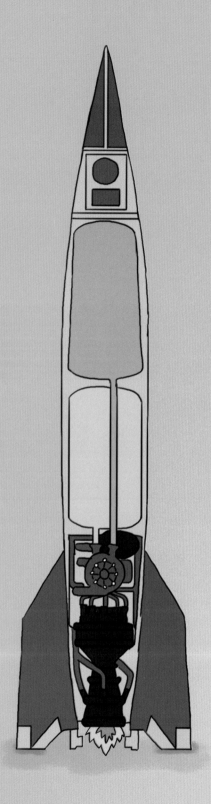

Thanks to the creative team:

Senior Editor: Alice Peebles
Fact checking: Tom Jackson
Design: www.collaborate.agency

First published in Great Britain in 2019
by Hungry Tomato Ltd
PO Box 181
Edenbridge
Kent, TN8 9DP

Copyright © 2019 Hungry Tomato Ltd

A CIP catalogue record for this book is
available from the British Library.

ISBN 978-1-912108-30-5

Printed and bound in China

Discover more at
www.hungrytomato.com

INCREDIBLE INVENTIONS

by Matt Turner
Illustrated by Sarah Conner

HUNGRY TOMATO.

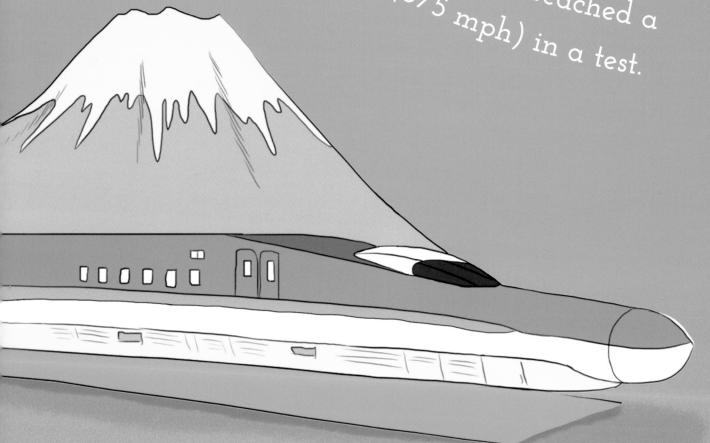

In 2015, a Japanese maglev (magnetic levitation) train reached a record 605 km/h (375 mph) in a test.

CONTENTS

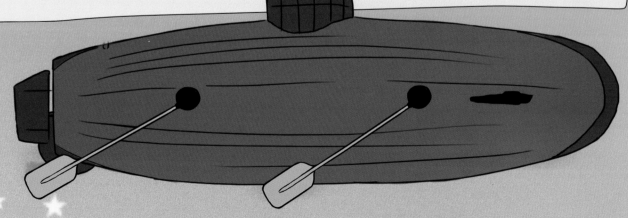

OFF WE GO!

We humans are natural wanderers, but for tens of thousands of years our ancestors moved on foot. So join us now on a journey by almost every craft you can think of, from dugout canoe to spacecraft. And meet the inventors who often risked their reputations, or even their lives, to test new hot-air balloons, gliders, parachutes, motorbikes, pushbikes, seaplanes, hovercraft... and even jetpacks and submarine-planes!

Spoked wheel, 2000 BCE

When our early ancestors first learned to make fire and control it, they altered human destiny. Come with us on a roundabout journey discovering all about light. From those early fire-making days to the modern era of lasers and satellite photography. We'll explore some of the more unexpected ways of looking at things – such as radio waves, microwaves, X rays and sound waves, which have given us radar and medical scanners.

And we'll poke 'light' fun at some of the crazier inventions people have dreamed up – such as spectacles for chickens and horses!

X-rays, 1895

The society we live in today is in a constant state of reinvention. *Incredible Inventions takes you through* the fascinating history of the inventions that have created our world, from earliest times, through the

turmoil of the industrial revolution, to modern day. Along the way, we'll look at what we eat (and how we grow it), the rise of steam power and electricity, keeping track of time, inventions around the home, medical milestones, smart manufacturing, and the creation of wonder materials like Velcro and Kevlar. And hopefully you'll spot that anyone – including you – can change the way we live today through a clever idea.

Medieval mouldboard plough, ninth century

iPhone, 2007

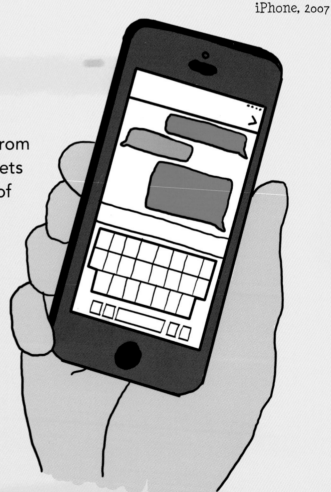

The history of communication takes us from earliest times to the invention of alphabets and writing, the printing press, the use of electricity in telegraph and telephone, right through to our modern digital age with its computers, satellites and smartphones.

Find out who invented paper and pens, printing, email and Instagram. And have fun with some hilarious predictions made by stick-in-the-muds who couldn't see any future for radio, television, cinema, the computer...

ON THE ROAD

The invention of the wheel revolutionized transport and technology, but it came fairly late in human history – maybe around 3000 BCE, long after humans had invented spears, flutes and pottery. In fact the idea came from the potter's wheel. The reason it took them so long is probably because there are no wheels in nature. This was a completely human invention.

PACK ANIMAL

Before we had wheels, we used pack animals. The onager or wild ass served as a beast of burden in ancient Sumer (modern Iraq).

FIRST WHEEL

The earliest wheels were solid planks, shaped and joined together. Carts like this one appeared in northern Europe in about 2500BCE. The cart is drawn by domestic cattle.

BENZ PATENT-MOTORWAGEN

In 1885, German inventor Karl Benz (later of Mercedes-Benz fame) produced the three-wheeled Patent-Motorwagen. His wife, Bertha, took it to visit her old mum, and on the way she invented brake lining.

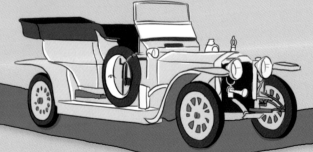

ROLLS-ROYCE

The Rolls-Royce 40/50 Silver Ghost appeared in 1907. A car magazine called it 'the best car in the world'; it was also the most expensive.

MODEL T

American Henry Ford designed his Model T car in 1908. In 1913, he invented the production line: cars were built in a strict sequence – three cars per minute!

SPOKED WHEELS

The Andronovo people, riding their chariots on the Eurasian plains 4,000 years ago, are thought to have invented spokes. Spokes made wheels lighter, bigger and faster.

STAGECOACH

The coach was invented in Koc (pronounced 'kotch'), Hungary. In 17th-century Europe, long journeys were made by stagecoach. Early models gave a bumpy ride, but by 1800, coaches were fast and comfy, with sprung suspension and brakes.

STEAM ENGINE

Steam engines, used in boats from the 1780s, and later in railway locos, also began to power road vehicles. The 'Obedient' was a steam carriage made by Frenchman Amédée Bollée in 1875.

HIPPOMOBILE

In the late 1850s, Étienne Lenoir of Belgium invented a gas-powered engine, and later used it in his Hippomobile (meaning 'horse car', not 'hippo car'). Its top speed was 3 km/h (1.8 mph) — slower than walking pace.

Need a push?

Volkswagen means 'people's car'. By 2003, more than 21 million Beetles had been sold.

Hmm, what shall I call it?

BEETLE

Porsche of Germany make luxury sportscars. But back in the 1930s, Ferdinand Porsche also designed the very affordable Volkswagen Beetle — named after its bug-like shape.

11

THE IC ENGINE

The internal combustion (IC) engine is fuelled by petrol, diesel or gas. Fuel explosions in the cylinders give out energy, which creates movement to turn the wheels. The IC engine appeared over 150 years ago, with many improvements added since.

THE FOUR-STROKE CYCLE

Camshaft   Spark plug

Valves

Piston

Crankshaft   Cylinder

1. Fuel/air mix enters cylinder.

2. Piston rises, squeezing fuel/air mix.

3. Spark plug ignites fuel, forcing cylinder down.

4. Piston returns, pushing exhaust (burnt gas) out.

CARBURETTOR

Fuel is vaporized inside the carburettor (right, which works a bit like an old-fashioned perfume spray). The fuel mist then enters the cylinder heads, where it is ignited by the spark plugs. The first effective carburettors were invented in the 1880s.

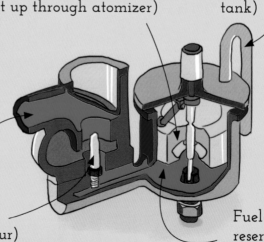

Float (presses on fuel, forcing it up through atomizer)

Fuel intake (from fuel tank)

Fuel vapour (to cylinders)

Atomizer jet (turns fuel from a liquid into vapour)

Fuel reservoir

GAS ENGINE

Remember Étienne Lenoir and the hippo car? This is his 1850s engine. The fuel was coal gas, which in those days was used for street lighting. But around that time, we began converting crude oil into paraffin, kerosene and petrol. Petrol became the preferred engine fuel.

> I shall call it... Diesel!

DIESEL ENGINE

In 1892-97, German Rudolf Diesel invented and improved the engine that bears his name. His first diesel engine was seven times more efficient than steam engines: it produced more power from less fuel.

A V8 engine has eight cylinders. They are arranged in a V-shape, with two blocks of four.

V8 ENGINE

Frenchman Léon Levavasseur invented the V8 engine in 1902, naming it the 'Antoinette' (after the daughter of his sponsor). It was mostly used in planes. This 1905 Darracq racing car had a 22.5-litre V8. It broke the land speed record!

> Va... Va... Vrooooom!

ON TWO WHEELS

It's hard to imagine a world without bikes, isn't it? But they were only invented about 200 years ago. The first 'bone-shakers' were wood and iron, and very hard on the bum. Motorbikes, too, began as very crude machines, around 150 years ago.

DRAISINE

The wooden *Draisine* of 1817 was named after its German inventor, Karl von Drais. It had no pedals, so he called it a 'running machine'.

VELOCIPEDE

The French Michauline, or velocipede, of the 1860s was designed by Pierre Lallement and Pierre Michaux. It had no tyres but the seat was sprung.

PETROL CYCLE

Englishman Edward Butler invented the three-wheeled Petrol Cycle in 1884. But its top speed of 16 km/h (10 mph) excluded it from built-up areas; the city speed limit was 3 km/h (2 mph)!

REITWAGEN

The Reitwagen, made by Gottlieb Daimler and Wilhelm Maybach, was the first true motorcycle, in 1885. But its seat caught fire. Ouch!

EARLY MOTORBIKE

Hildebrand & Wolfmüller, Germany, 1894 – one of the first reliable motorbikes

TRIUMPH

The Triumph Type H, England, 1915, used by messengers in World War I

Bye guys!

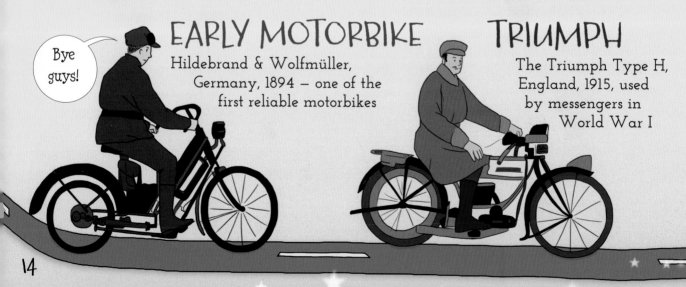

PENNY-FARTHING

The 'ordinary' of the 1870s was also called a 'penny-farthing', because its wheels looked like two coins — one small, one large.

Oops!

SAFETY BIKE

Penny-farthings were very hard to ride, and crashed a lot. They were replaced later by 'safety bicycles'. This is the Rover safety bicycle of 1885, made by Englishman John Starley.

HELMET

The lid that saves lives... After famous British soldier T. E. Lawrence died in a motorbike crash in 1935, doctors began calling for the use of crash helmets. In America, racing driver Rory Richter was inspired to launch the Bell helmet brand in the 1950s, after a friend died in a crash.

MICHAUX

The Michaux steam-powered bike of 1867 was basically a Michauline push-bike with a steam engine attached.

VESPA

Vespa MP-6 'moped', Italy, 1946 — a motor scooter for everyone

HONDA

Honda CB750, 1969 — one of the first modern, fast Japanese bikes

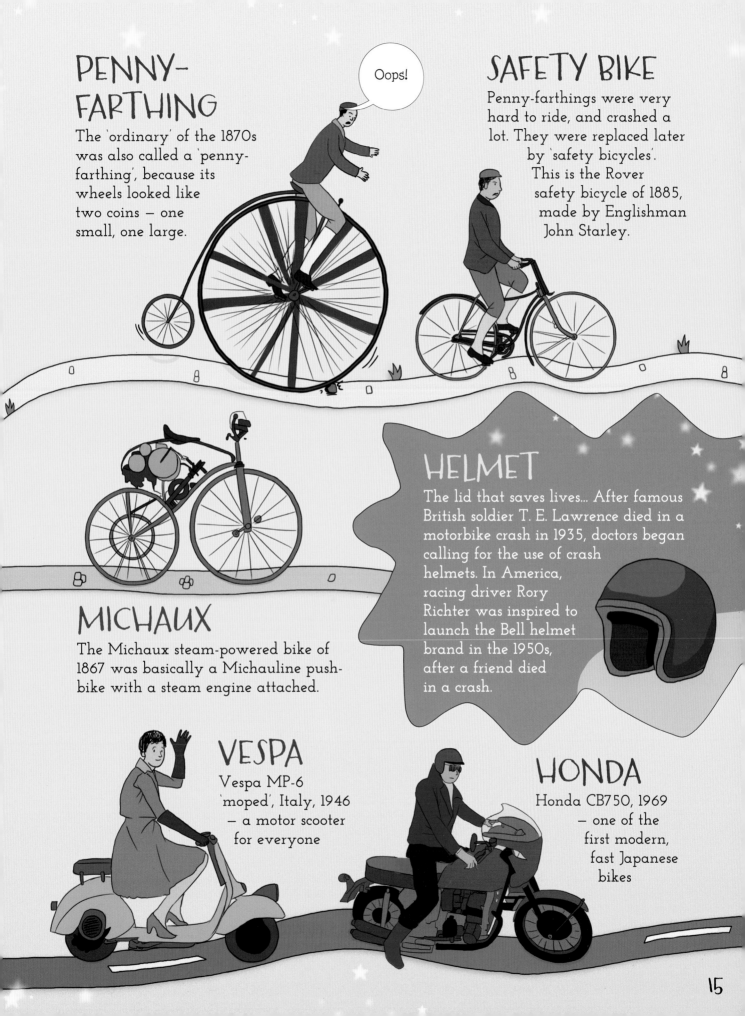

THE FIRST BOATS

Since paddling the very first fallen log across a creek, we humans have been steadily improving watercraft design. Sails were first used by the Mesopotamians some 5,000 years ago, but the invention of the triangular lateen sail, about 1,800 years ago, enabled mariners to put to sea in almost any wind. As shipping evolved, so did sea power and trade.

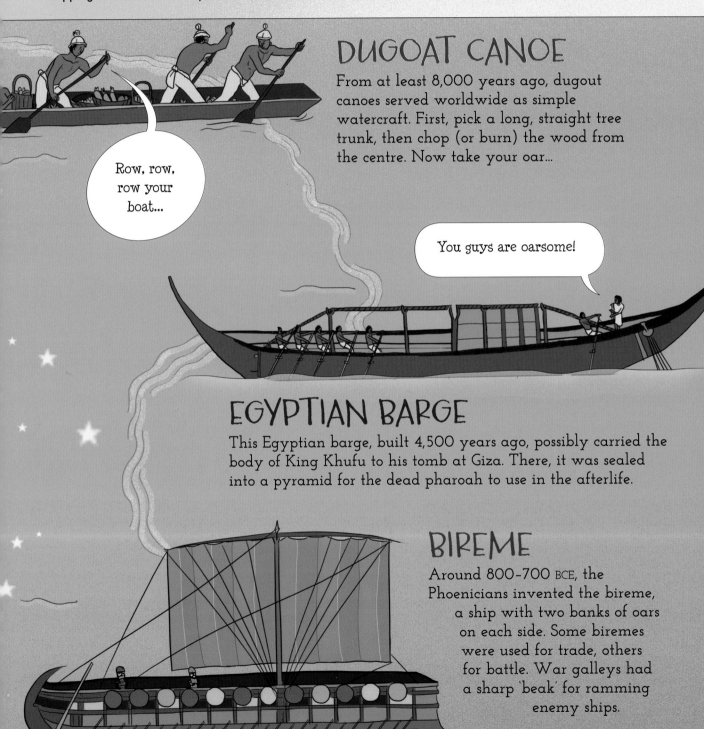

DUGOAT CANOE

From at least 8,000 years ago, dugout canoes served worldwide as simple watercraft. First, pick a long, straight tree trunk, then chop (or burn) the wood from the centre. Now take your oar...

Row, row, row your boat...

You guys are oarsome!

EGYPTIAN BARGE

This Egyptian barge, built 4,500 years ago, possibly carried the body of King Khufu to his tomb at Giza. There, it was sealed into a pyramid for the dead pharoah to use in the afterlife.

BIREME

Around 800-700 BCE, the Phoenicians invented the bireme, a ship with two banks of oars on each side. Some biremes were used for trade, others for battle. War galleys had a sharp 'beak' for ramming enemy ships.

Beak

AIRCRAFT CARRIERS

Modern aircraft carriers are gigantic to allow aircraft to take off. Some have measured up to 333 m (1,092 ft) long and carried up to 90 aircraft. This ship is painted in dazzle camouflage.

1826 propellor designed by Czech inventor Josef Ressel

PROPELLERS

Ships' propellers were invented in the early 1800s. Paddle wheels are much older; the Romans even had paddle ships powered by cows!

WIND POWER

The caravel was a 15th-century Portuguese ship whose triangular lateen sails allowed it to sail in almost any wind direction. This example is the *Matthew*, in which explorer John Cabot crossed the Atlantic in 1497.

GIANT JUNKS

From 1405 to 1423, Chinese traders and explorers mounted sea expeditions as far west as Africa. Under the command of Admiral Zheng He, they sailed in huge fleets of sailing ships known as junks, some 122 m (400 ft) long — among the largest wooden ships ever built. They were often called 'treasure ships'.

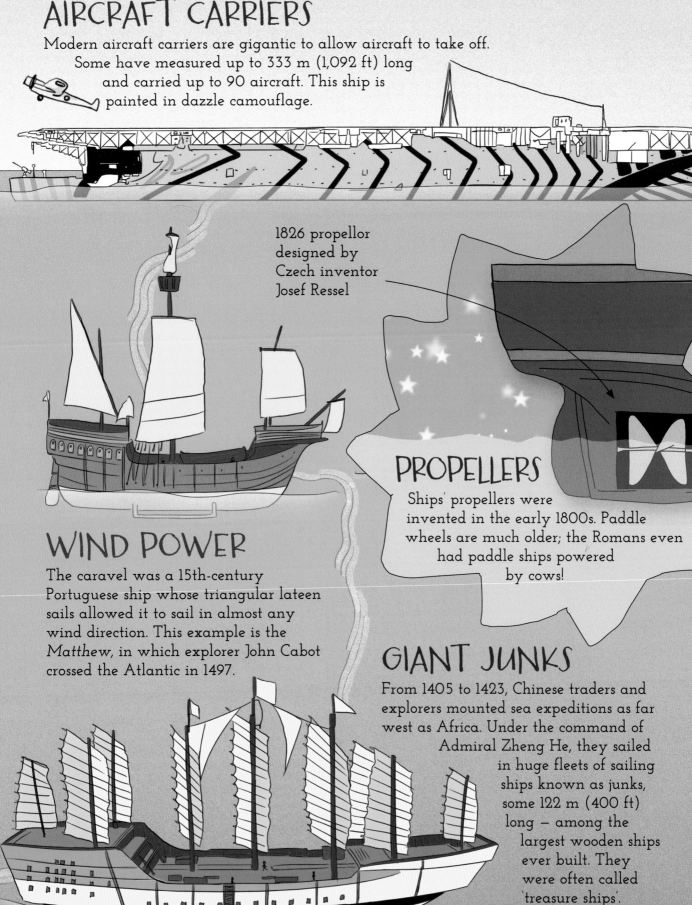

WATER WONDERS

Why travel on the water when you can go under it? The history of the submarine dates back 400 years – but you wouldn't want to try some of those ancient leaky tubs! Or perhaps a hovercraft is what really floats your boat?

OUTBOARD MOTOR

This 1902 French outboard motor made steering tricky – like using a giant egg-beater! The first serious outboard was made in 1907 by Norwegian-born Ole Evinrude.

HOVERCRAFT

In 1959, Christopher Cockerell crossed the English Channel in his first full-size hovercraft, the SR.N1. His design borrowed ideas from hovercraft research dating back to the 1870s.

SUB WITH OARS

Cornelius Drebbel was a brilliant Dutchman whose many inventions included a submarine with oars. In 1624, he showed his latest sub to King James I of England, and even took the monarch for a ride in the River Thames!

TURTLE

In 1775, American David Bushnell designed the *Turtle*, a one-man submarine. He wanted to use it to place explosives secretly on British ships during the Revolutionary War.

I've sunk so low, solo...

18

GROUND EFFECT

Ground-effect aeroplanes float several metres above water on a cushion of trapped air. This huge Lun aeroplane, built in Russia in the 1960s, measured over 90 m (300 ft) long. It was unstable, though, so the idea didn't really 'take off'.

JETBOATS

Jetboats were invented by New Zealander Bill Hamilton in the 1950s. The engine scoops up water from below and pumps it out the back to push the boat forward.

HOLLAND 1

This is the British Royal Navy's *Holland 1* submarine of 1901, designed by Irish engineer John Holland. She sank off the British coast in 1913 while being towed, and was lost. In 1983 she was recovered and restored for museum display.

Holland 1 measured nearly 20 m (64 ft) long and was armed with one torpedo tube.

RAIL TRAIL

Powerful, high-pressure steam engines, invented in the 1800s, soon found their way onto the railways – although the earliest locomotives were very slow puffers! Since then, diesel and electric locos, and even 'magnetic levitation' trains, have drawn the railway into the modern era, providing us with fast, smooth, mass transport.

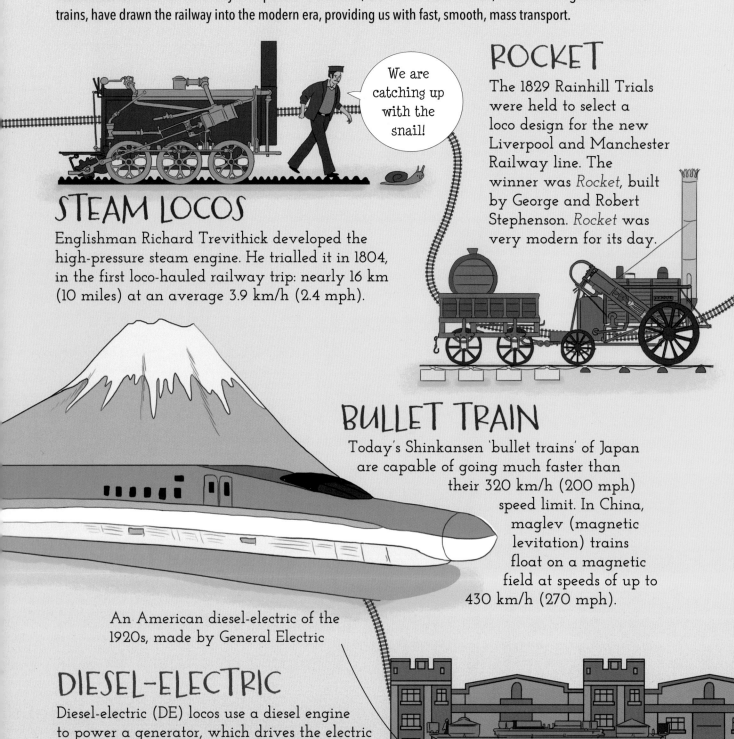

We are catching up with the snail!

STEAM LOCOS

Englishman Richard Trevithick developed the high-pressure steam engine. He trialled it in 1804, in the first loco-hauled railway trip: nearly 16 km (10 miles) at an average 3.9 km/h (2.4 mph).

ROCKET

The 1829 Rainhill Trials were held to select a loco design for the new Liverpool and Manchester Railway line. The winner was *Rocket*, built by George and Robert Stephenson. *Rocket* was very modern for its day.

BULLET TRAIN

Today's Shinkansen 'bullet trains' of Japan are capable of going much faster than their 320 km/h (200 mph) speed limit. In China, maglev (magnetic levitation) trains float on a magnetic field at speeds of up to 430 km/h (270 mph).

An American diesel-electric of the 1920s, made by General Electric

DIESEL-ELECTRIC

Diesel-electric (DE) locos use a diesel engine to power a generator, which drives the electric motor that moves the train. When DEs replaced smoky old steam trains in city areas, it helped keep laundry clean!

ELECTRIC TRAIN

In 1879, German inventor Werner von Siemens built this little electric train — the world's first. (The next year, he built the first electric elevator; and the year after that, the first electric tramway, in Berlin.)

Ermm, it's a little bit small.

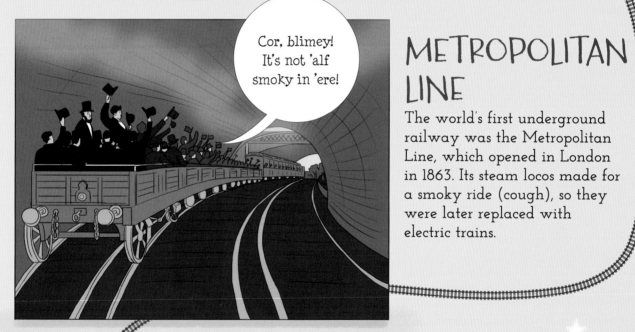

Cor, blimey! It's not 'alf smoky in 'ere!

METROPOLITAN LINE

The world's first underground railway was the Metropolitan Line, which opened in London in 1863. Its steam locos made for a smoky ride (cough), so they were later replaced with electric trains.

Choo-choo coming through!

MALLARD

The British *Mallard*, designed by Sir Nigel Gresley in 1938, still holds the world steam speed record of just over 202 km/h (125 mph). Its beautiful streamlining creates a sleek, slippery shape, keeping wind resistance low.

FIRST FLIGHT

You look at the birds and you want to fly too, right? You're not the first. The earliest attempts go back as far as ancient China. But it was the development of hot-air balloons just over two centuries ago, and much later the dawn of powered, controlled flight, that turned human dreams of flight into a reality.

CHINESE KITE

As much as 3,000 years ago, Chinese 'aviators' flew strapped to big kites. Later, sailors would send manned kites up into the air to test the prospects for a good voyage.

Hey, you down there... don't let go of that string!

LEONARDO'S MACHINE

The Italian artist-genius Leonardo da Vinci (1452-1519) invented a flying machine inspired by bats and birds, though he never actually built it. (He also invented helicopters — on paper, at least!)

FLOATPLANE

Floatplanes, or seaplanes, are aircraft that can take off from water, and land on it, too. They date from 1905, when French aircraft pioneer Gabriel Voisin piloted a float-glider over the River Seine. It was towed by a speedboat.

HOT-AIR BALLOON

France, 19 September 1783: the two Montgolfier brothers launch a hot-air balloon carrying a sheep, a duck and a rooster. The animals returned safely. Later that year, the Montgolfiers launched the world's first manned flights.

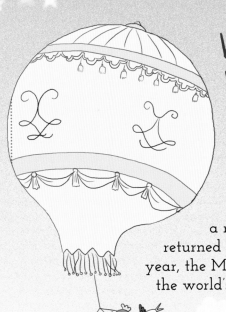

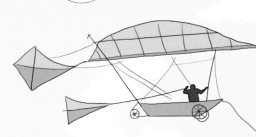

Baa... ooh-ah!

GAS BURNER

The Montgolfiers lit a fire under their balloons to lift them. In 1955, American Ed Yost introduced the on-board gas burner. In 1978, Yost's *Double Eagle II* made the first balloon crossing of the Atlantic Ocean.

GLIDER

British inventor George Cayley sent a glider up in 1853, piloted by one of his servants (who, luckily, came down again unharmed).

AIRSHIP

This huge airship, which first flew in July 1900, was named after its German inventor, Count Ferdinand von Zeppelin. His first Zeppelin, the *LZ1*, measured 128 m (420 ft) — nearly three times the length of a modern jumbo jet.

AIR POWER

Next time you're in a plane, it'll probably be a comfy jet airliner with in-flight food, and maybe also movies. But only a century ago, planes were flimsy craft of 'stick, string and fabric', with little more than hope and courage to keep them in the air.

JET AIRCRAFT

The first jet planes also appeared in World War II. They were invented by Hans von Ohain in Germany and Frank Whittle in Britain. The Heinkel He178, powered by a von Ohain engine, made the world's first jet flight in 1939.

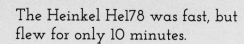

The Heinkel He178 was fast, but flew for only 10 minutes.

Spitfire. Lives up to its name. Better than Shrew, eh.

SPITFIRE

The British Supermarine Spitfire, designed in 1936 by Reg Mitchell, was a famous World War II fighter plane with wing-mounted guns. Mitchell originally wanted to call it 'Shrew' or 'Scarab', and didn't like 'Spitfire'. More than 20,000 Spitfires were built; about 50 still fly today.

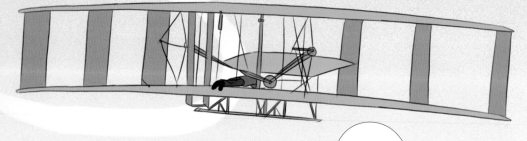

It flies!

WRIGHT BROTHERS

Wilbur and Orville Wright made the world's first powered flights at Kitty Hawk, North Carolina, in 1903. They had begun building gliders, but their first powered plane, the *Flyer 1*, carried a 12-horsepower motor.

CONCORDE

The beautiful British-French Concorde served as an airliner between 1976 and 2003. It carried up to 128 passengers at over twice the speed of sound. The long nose could be 'drooped' on landing so that the pilot could see over it!

EJECTION SEAT

The ejection seat saves pilots' lives by throwing them from a stricken plane before it crashes. Its inventors include the British company Martin-Baker.

If a plane gets into trouble, the pilot triggers the ejection sequence. First, the canopy opens rapidly.

The seat is quickly blown out by rocket or jet power, lifting the pilot high above the plane.

The parachute opens to carry the pilot safely back to land.

The VS-300 was the first helicopter to use a tail rotor successfully.

Leonardo da Vinci thought of that first!

HELICOPTER

In 1907 Paul Cornu, a bicycle maker, made the first manned helicopter flight, but his experimental craft rose only a few feet. The first truly successful heli was the VS-300, designed in 1939 by Russian-American Igor Sikorsky.

SPACE TRAVEL

If you want to explore space, jets and IC engines are not up to the job. You need a rocket. Large rockets are powerful enough to escape Earth's gravity, and carry all their own fuel and oxygen. Space travel is only a few decades old, but was predicted much earlier by scientists and sci-fi fantasy writers.

CHINESE ROCKET

Basic rocket science is this: the engine exhaust pushes backwards to push the rocket forwards. The Chinese grasped this when they invented gunpowder.

MEN ON THE MOON

On the Apollo 15 mission (1971), US astronauts David Scott and Jim Irwin spent three days on the Moon. They travelled the surface in this electric Lunar Roving Vehicle (LRV).

Back in 1903, Tsiolkovsky predicted the use of multi-stage rockets with disposable booster sections.

ROCKET SCIENCE

Russian Konstantin Tsiolkovsky (1857–1935) worked out a lot of the tricky maths in rocket science. Although he himself never built a rocket, his work was an inspiration for later pioneers in Germany and America.

LIQUID-FUEL ROCKET

On 16 March 1926, American scientist Robert Goddard launched the world's first liquid-fuel rocket. It rose to 12 m (41 ft), then crash-landed in his Aunt Effie's cabbage patch. But he had made history.

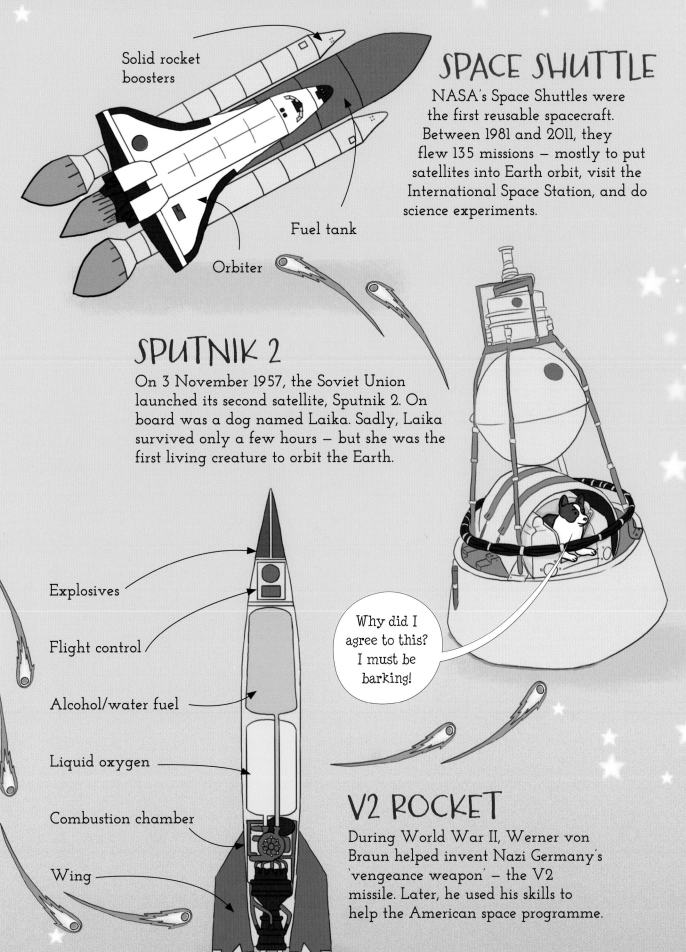

SPACE SHUTTLE

NASA's Space Shuttles were the first reusable spacecraft. Between 1981 and 2011, they flew 135 missions — mostly to put satellites into Earth orbit, visit the International Space Station, and do science experiments.

Solid rocket boosters

Fuel tank

Orbiter

SPUTNIK 2

On 3 November 1957, the Soviet Union launched its second satellite, Sputnik 2. On board was a dog named Laika. Sadly, Laika survived only a few hours — but she was the first living creature to orbit the Earth.

Why did I agree to this? I must be barking!

Explosives

Flight control

Alcohol/water fuel

Liquid oxygen

Combustion chamber

Wing

V2 ROCKET

During World War II, Werner von Braun helped invent Nazi Germany's 'vengeance weapon' — the V2 missile. Later, he used his skills to help the American space programme.

27

NAVIGATION

Travellers need to know where they are, and where they're going. Finding your way around is called navigating. In early times, this was tricky enough on land, but doubly difficult at sea – at least, until the invention of maps, charts, logs, compasses and other navigational aids.

ERATOSTHENES
HIPPARCHUS

Eratosthenes calculated the circumference of the Earth by measuring shadows cast by the sun. Clever guy!

LATITUDE AND LONGITUDE

Maps have lines of latitude (east-west around the Earth) and longitude (north-south, through the poles). The ancient Greeks Eratosthenes and Hipparchus 'invented' latitude and longitude.

CHARTS

Sailors' sea maps are called charts. Italian mariners of the 13th century made the first 'portulan' charts, which showed lines of the compass marking out routes for traders and explorers.

10... 11... 12... 13... How long do I have to count for?

SHIP'S LOG

A ship's log measures speed through water. The earliest one really was a log, to which was tied a rope with knots along its length. Sailors threw the log overboard and counted the knots passing through their hands. That's why a ship's speed is measured in knots.

GPS

These days, mariners have GPS (the Global Positioning System), which uses satellite data to create very accurate electronic charts. The US Department of Defense invented GPS, and 'switched it on' in 1995.

SEA WATCH

If you could keep time at sea, you could work out your position. This H4 'sea watch' of 1761 had taken English clockmaker John Harrison six years to make. Captain James Cook took an H4 watch on his famous voyages to the Pacific.

Harrison's watches were very expensive – roughly one-third of the total cost of fitting out a ship!

QUADRANT

Sailors have long used the stars to navigate by. This 18th-century seaman is using a Davis quadrant to look back at the sun and measure its angle.

FIRST COMPASS

The ancient Chinese invented the compass: a magnetite pointer on a bronze plate. By the 10th century, they'd worked out how to magnetize needles, making better compasses that helped their trading ships navigate at sea.

MAKING LIGHT

You probably have an electric light on right now, don't you? Flicked it on with a switch? Our ancestors weren't so lucky: they used all sorts of tricks, from rubbing sticks together to making matches or giant batteries, all in order to create light.

It's got oil lamp headlights...

FIRE

Around a million years ago, our early ancestors learnt to make fire by rubbing sticks, so creating heat by friction. They also struck sparks from hard stones. Remains of burnt bones show that they cooked meat.

OIL LAMPS

Oil lamps date back more than 12,000 years. They were often made from shells or carved stone, or just a clay cup, using animal fat for fuel. Roman lamps ran on olive oil, and some had 10 or 12 wicks each.

LIGHTHOUSES

The Pharos ('light') of Alexandria in Egypt, built over 2,000 years ago, stood nearly 137 m (450 ft) tall, until it was toppled centuries later by earthquakes. A furnace at the top of the Pharos produced the light. Later lighthouses used light bulbs, thanks to Edison's smart idea (right).

MATCHES

The Chinese invented matches about 1,000 years ago, naming them 'fire inch-sticks'. Reliable friction matches — lit by scraping on sandpaper — first appeared in Britain in the 1820s. These early matches contained phosphorus, which made match factory workers — and sellers, like this boy — very sick.

INCANDESCENT LIGHT

British scientist Humphry Davy invented incandescent light (that is, light resulting from heat) in 1802. He heated a strip of platinum till it glowed, using the world's (then) most powerful battery: 2,000 linked cells. Wow!

I say, do you have this battery in a pocket torch size?

Hey, I have a great idea...

DAVY'S SAFETY LAMP

Davy is famous for inventing a 'safety lamp' in 1815, for use by coal miners. Its flame was covered over, to reduce the risk of gas explosions. It didn't work too well: the light was dim, and the explosions continued. Humph!

EDISON'S GREAT IDEA

American Thomas Edison didn't invent the first light bulb, but in 1879 he came up with the first reliable one — after testing more than 3,000 bulb designs and about 6,000 different filaments! (The filament is the glowing thread inside.)

SEEING NEAR

Magnifying glasses, spectacles, contact lenses and microscopes all rely on the fact that a curved piece of glass – a lens – focuses light and makes things look closer than they are. Through history, lenses have led to many scientific discoveries (as well as giving us one more thing to lose on the bus).

Carrots, frogs' legs, milk...

MAGNIFIER

Before magnifying glasses existed, the ancient Romans just filled a glass bowl with water. Looking through it, they saw things at larger size.

SPECTACLES

Early Arabs knew about optics, but in the West, English monk Roger Bacon was the first to write about lenses, in 1268. Within 20 years, the Italians had invented 'clip-on' specs.

I wish I couldn't see these frogs' legs.

BIFOCALS

American statesman Benjamin Franklin (1706-90) invented bifocals: spectacles with lenses of two different strengths. On a trip to France, he used them to see both his dinner and fellow-diners.

CONTACT LENSES

In 1888, German doctor Adolf Fick designed the earliest practical contact lenses. He first tested them on rabbits. (But how did he tell that they worked?!)

How many carrots am I holding up?

ELECTRON MICROSCOPE

Super-powerful scanning electron microscopes (SEMs) were invented in the 1930s by German TV engineer Max Knoll. SEMs were first used to look closely at metals. They also take terrifying pictures of bugs...

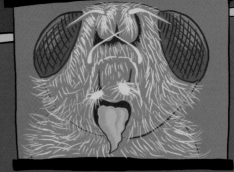

...and this is a house fly's tongue!

Ewww!

Eye piece

Ancient Greek-style 'water lamp' for illumination

Lens barrel

Specimen holder

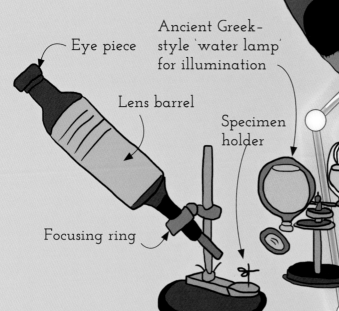

Focusing ring

HOOKE'S MICROSCOPE

Englishman Robert Hooke was the first to use the word 'cell' to describe the basic unit of life. He looked at cells through his microscope of 1665.

SEEING THE INVISIBLE

A microscope uses really powerful lenses to make truly tiny things look big. The first were compound microscopes: tubes with sets of lenses that worked together to magnify. With these, scientists saw bacteria, blood cells and yeast for the first time.

Main screw

Focusing screw

Specimen pin

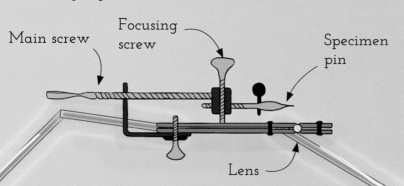

Lens

This 'scope (top view below, side view left) was designed by Dutchman Antonie van Leeuwenhoek (1632-1723). You put a specimen on a sharp point and viewed it through the 275x lens mounted in the plate.

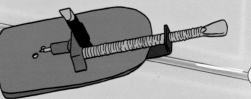

SEEING FAR

Telescopes aren't just for spying on your neighbours: they've enabled astronomers to look deep into space and make discoveries about planets, moons and stars. Early telescopes used lenses, rather like microscopes, but today we also use radio telescopes to explore the universe.

EARLY TELESCOPE

Dutchman Hans Lippershey made magnifiers and ran a spectacles shop. In 1608, he came up with an early telescope, which he called a 'looker'. He offered it to the government to use in battle; they promised him a reward if he converted them into binoculars!

ARGH! They are so close!

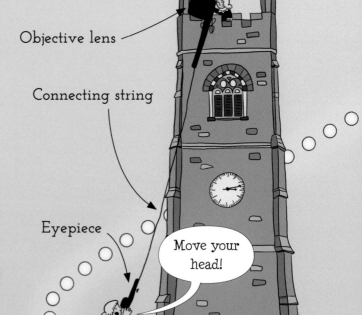

Objective lens

Connecting string

Eyepiece

Move your head!

AERIAL TELESCOPE

In the 1600s, the Dutch brothers Christiaan and Constantine Huygens made giant 'aerial' telescopes, which had no tubing. They mounted one lens near the ground, and the other on a tall support.

OBSERVING SPACE

Italian scientist Galileo Galilei (1564-1642) famously built his own telescopes to study the skies, where he discovered four of Jupiter's moons (among other things). He also used them to study insects. His telescopes were so handy, he sold a few to seafarers.

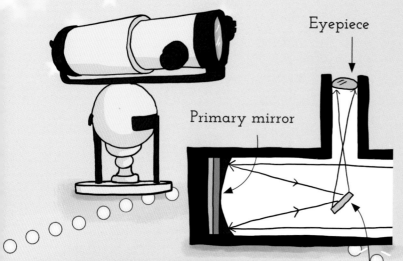

Eyepiece

Primary mirror

FINDING SATURN'S MOONS

In 1789, German–British astronomer William Herschel built this 12-m-long (40-ft) giant. It was a reflecting 'scope, like Newton's, but with an improved mirror set-up. He used it to look at Saturn's moons. One of them, Mimas, looks scarily like the Death Star...

REFLECTING TELESCOPE

Secondary mirror

Early telescope lenses tended to split light into rainbow colours, making images hard to see. British scientist Isaac Newton fixed this problem in 1668 with a reflecting telescope. This used a mirror, not a lens, to capture the image.

RADIO TELESCOPE

Modern radio telescopes don't 'look' with lenses, but 'listen' like TV antennae. American Karl Jansky built the first radio telescope in a potato field in 1931. He attached antennae to a radio receiver to detect radio waves from space — energy from star activity — which he heard as a steady hiss.

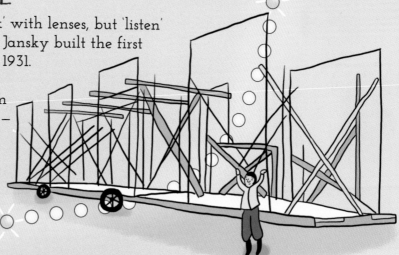

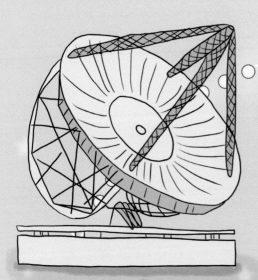

RADIO ASTRONOMY

Jansky's discovery inspired Grote Reber, a fellow American, to build a radio telescope in his back garden in 1937. Reber used it to create a 'map' of space radio signals. In those early years, he was the world's only radio astronomer! Today there are thousands...

THE CAMERA

Cameras are amazingly complex today, but the basic idea comes from the 'camera obscura' (meaning 'darkened room'), or pinhole camera. This is a box, with the only light coming from a small hole in one wall. Light enters and, like a film projector, casts an image (upside down) on the opposite wall. If you line that wall with photosensitive film or paper, you capture the image as a photograph.

CAMERA OBSCURA

The Arab scientist Alhazen (965-1040) described how pinhole cameras worked. Astronomers and artists took up the idea.

PHOTOGRAPHIC PAPER PICTURES

Around 1800, British scientist Thomas Wedgwood experimented with photosensitive paper. He left it on sunny windowsills, taking 'shadow photos' of leaves and other objects.

EARLY PHOTOGRAPHY

The true inventors of photography were Frenchmen Nicéphore Niépce and Louis Daguerre. Nic tried photosensitive chemicals (silver chloride, bitumen, lavender oil) and began taking basic photos around 1816. In 1839, Daguerre developed the 'daguerreotype' method. This used a polished silver sheet coated with chemicals and exposed to light in a camera obscura called, yep, a 'Daguerre' (below). It took very sharp photographs.

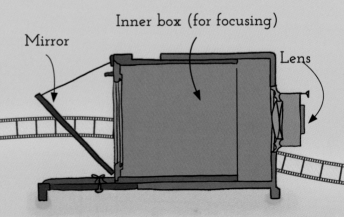

Inner box (for focusing)

Mirror

Lens

Say cheese!

POLAROID PICTURES

The Polaroid camera takes pictures you can instantly print. It was invented in 1947 by American Edwin Land.

DIGITAL CAMERAS

The invention of the charge-coupled device (CCD), an electronic gizmo, by Willard Smith and Bill Boyle in 1969 led to the end of film and the dawn of the digital camera, invented in 1975 by Stephen Sasson.

EASTMAN KODAK

The big revolution in photography came with the invention of film by American George Eastman in 1884. It featured in his Kodak camera, which he patented in 1888. The invention of small, affordable cameras, such as the Brownie, meant that, from now on, anyone could be a photographer.

POSITIVE AND NEGATIVE

Also in the 1830s, British scientist William Fox Talbot came up with the calotype: a better, faster method than the daguerrotype. With the calotype, you could make a negative – a 'back to front' image – and use this to make positive copies.

SURVEYING

Surveying means measuring the land. It is important because it gives us maps and GPS (which stops mum and dad getting lost when driving). It also led surveyors on some exciting and dangerous journeys.

MEASURING MOUNTAINS

Ancient Egyptians used long, knotted ropes for measuring distances. Early Chinese (below) used a protractor on a pole to calculate mountain heights by measuring angles. This method, or versions of it, saw use for many centuries.

I'm sure it's around here somewhere...

FIRST MAP

Here is the first known map of the world: the Imago Mundi from Babylon (in modern-day Iraq). An unknown person scratched it onto a clay tablet some 2,500 years ago. The ring represents the ocean, surrounding the lands.

SATELLITE IMAGING

Nowadays, satellites orbiting Earth take photos so clear, they can spot you sunbathing in the garden. Explorer 6, launched in 1959, took some of the first photos from space. They were very fuzzy — but it was the dawn of satellite imaging.

THEODOLITES

To chart new empires, surveyors went out with theodolites. These were basically telescopes that measured angles very accurately. Some were huge, like this one built by Jesse Ramsden in England in the 1780s, weighing nearly 100 kg (22 lb). And in the young US, the young George Washington was the first surveyor of northern Virginia...

AERIAL PHOTOGRAPHY

Frenchman Nadar launched aerial photography in 1858. This was his biggest balloon, named The Giant. He also invented airmail! During 1870-71, he used a fleet of balloons to smuggle more than 2,000,000 messages out of Paris, which was under siege by the Germans.

RECONNAISSANCE

Maul's 'rocket-cam' never really took off, because very soon aerial photographers were using planes. First off was Wilbur Wright (pioneer of flight), in 1909. In World War I, enemy positions were recorded in this way by both sides.

ROCKET CAMERAS

Swedish genius Alfred Nobel (famous for the Nobel Prize) pioneered aerial photography from rockets in 1897. In 1906, German engineer Albert Maul (right) built a more efficient design, powered by compressed air.

I hope I remembered the film!

MAKING MOVIES

Who doesn't love watching movies? Your great-great-grandparents, that's who. After all, the film camera is still quite young, having first appeared in the 1890s. But long before then, inventors had begun to make clever toys that tricked our eyes into thinking we were looking at moving pictures… movies.

PHENAKISTOSCOPE

One toy was the phenakistoscope of 1832, invented by Belgian Joseph Plateau. It had two discs, one ringed with pictures. You spun the discs, looked through a slot at a mirror, and saw the pictures 'join up' and move.

ZOOPRAXISCOPE

Similar toys included the zoopraxiscope (Eadweard Muybridge, 1879). It made the first moving photographic image.

FIRST MOVIE CAMERA

Some claim that Thomas Edison invented the movie camera — but the true pioneer was France's Louis Le Prince. He used this camera (right) to shoot some film in Leeds, England, in 1888. Two years later he disappeared, so he never got rich from his invention.

Come on — hurry up!

KINETOGRAPH

Edison and his helper Bill Dickson did invent a movie camera called the Kinetograph. And in 1891 he unveiled the Kinetoscope projector, which showed movies. But only one person at a time could use it.

VCR TECHNOLOGY

Nowadays you can watch movies on a smartphone. A generation ago, your mum and dad watched them with a VCR, which is short for 'video cassette recorder'. The first VCR was made by Russian-American Alex Poniatoff and his Ampex company. It was so huge you couldn't even carry it, let alone tuck it in your pocket.

MOVIEMAKERS

The first true moviemakers were French brothers Auguste and Louis Lumière. In 1895, they filmed their workers leaving the factory, then gave a public screening of – guess what they called it? – *Workers Leaving the Lumière Factory*. It sounds deadly boring, but viewers were amazed (even though these first films had no sound at all).

VIEWING IN 3D

3D movies are great fun. But they, like the old phenakistoscope, are simply clever tricks that fool your brain. And you might think that making and viewing three-dimensional pictures is new, but it's more than 150 years old – older, even, than the movie camera.

STEREOSCOPE

3D pictures date back almost to the invention of photography. The Brewster Stereoscope of 1849 held two photos – left and right – each taken from a slightly different spot. Viewed together, they gave a 3D effect.

Eyepiece

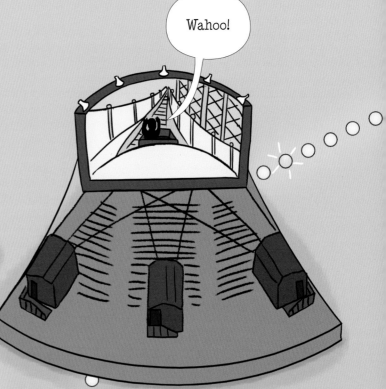
Wahoo!

3D PROJECTOR

Alfred Molteni, an Italian-French optician, used a special slide projector with two lenses to create a 3D effect. This audience is watching his nature slides.

Ahh!

CINERAMA

A more modern, movie version of Molteni's rig was Cinerama, invented by American Fred Waller. It used a huge, curved cinema screen, with a 'joined-up' picture created by three film projectors. At the first viewing in 1952, people were so excited, they screamed! But Cinerama was hopelessly complicated and expensive until they worked out a way of using just one projector.

3D SCANNING

In 1859, at the circular studio of François Willème in Paris, you had your picture taken by 24 cameras mounted around the wall. Willème used a projector to copy each photo outline to a lump of clay, then carved it into a 3D 'photosculpture'. So 3D scanning and printing were born.

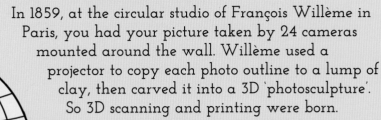

I love being the centre of attention!

SPECIAL EFFECTS

The modern version of Willème's rig, as used in the movie industry, is called 'photogrammetry'. Digital cameras take lots of scans of an actor, then animators use these to create special effects, which you watch at the movies.

APP SCAN

123D Catch, created in 2009 by Autodesk, takes 3D scans of objects, which can then be tinkered with on a computer, and even 3D-printed. Willème would have loved it!

43

SCANNING THE BODY

So far we've looked at bacteria, outer space, planet Earth… now it's time to look inside the body. Sounds gross? Maybe – but it saves millions of lives. Today it's called radiography, or radiology, because it uses the types of radiation wave that can pass through our bodies. Radiographers can also use sound waves to take pictures of our insides.

EARLY ENDOSCOPE

Around 1800, German doctor Philipp Bozzini invented his 'light conductor'. It had a candle and lens for looking right inside an ear or throat. It was one of the first endoscopes.

Oh my!

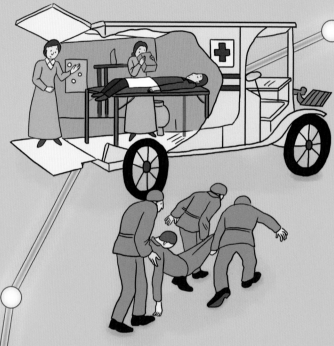

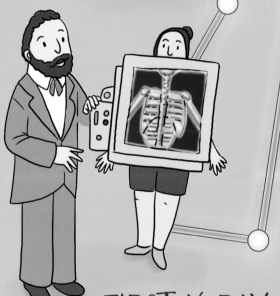

X-RAYS IN BATTLE

Scientists soon realized X-rays could be lifesavers. Polish-French chemist Marie Curie was a brilliant radiologist. During World War 1, she sent special medical trucks to the battlefields to take X-rays of wounded soldiers. She won many awards for her studies on radioactivity.

FIRST X-RAY

In Germany in 1895, Wilhelm Röntgen discovered that certain rays could pass straight through cardboard onto a screen, where they glowed. He took the first X-ray photograph, showing the bones in his wife Anna's hand.

CT SCANNER

The computerized tomography (CT) scanner, which looks a bit like a giant doughnut, photographs the body slice by slice. English engineer Godfrey Hounsfield invented it in the early 1970s. He tested it first on a dead human brain, then a cow's brain — then on himself!

Umm... cheese?

MRI

Armenian-American Raymond Damadian created MRI, or 'magnetic resonance imaging'. In 1977, Ray showed that, by measuring what happens to the potassium inside us when it is energized, a scanner can 'see' cancer tumours. Each year, radiologists take over 60 million MRI scans, helping to save countless lives.

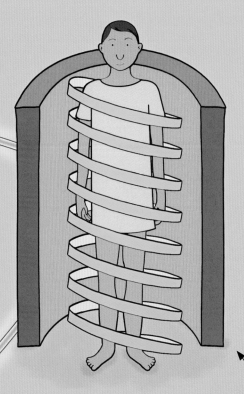

Ray's original sketch for an MRI machine looked a bit like this.

ULTRASOUND

Ian Donald and Tom Brown invented ultrasound in the 1950s for checking ships for flaws. Today it's used for checking babies before they're born.

PILLCAM

Digital cameras are now so tiny, you can even swallow one in a pill! The PillCam can spot problems in our gut as it passes through the digestive system. It was invented in 1997 by Israeli Gavriel Iddan. He had learnt his skills by working on guided missiles — rockets that find their own way to a target.

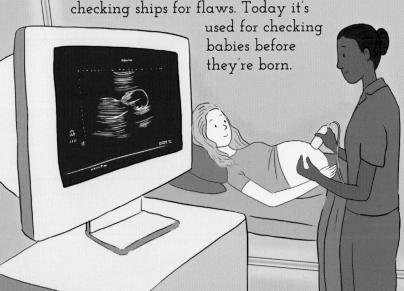

Pillcam

SONAR AND RADAR

Sonar is short for '**so**und **n**avigation **a**nd **r**anging'. It is a technology we've borrowed from nature: it creates pictures from sound waves as they echo off objects – rather as a bat catches moths, or a dolphin catches fish. Radar, too, picks up echoes, but it uses radio waves instead of sound.

SONAR EXPERIMENT

In 1822, Daniel Colladon and Charles Sturm used gunpowder and bells in a Swiss lake to measure how fast sound travelled in water. (It's four times faster than in air.) This was arguably the first sonar.

DISASTER AT SEA

In 1912, more than 1,500 passengers and crew died when the *Titanic* ocean liner sank. Experts later realized that, if the ship had been fitted with sonar, it would likely have seen the iceberg in its path, and avoided it.

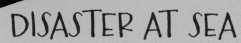

Chain Home radio masts

WARTIME RADAR

Scotsman Robert Watson-Watt helped develop radar ('**ra**dio **d**etection **a**nd **r**anging') into a war-winning technology. It was first used to help pilots detect thunderstorms.

Just before World War II, Watson-Watt proved that aircraft themselves could reflect radio waves. At his suggestion, Britain set up radar defences on the coast, called 'Chain Home', for detecting enemy aircraft up to 96 km (60 miles) away.

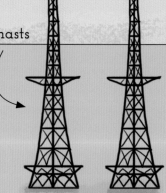

ICE DEVICE

Canadian engineer Reginald Fessenden designed a sonar system that could detect icebergs up to 3.2 km (2 miles) away, measure the sea's depth and send messages by Morse code. His invention was later fitted to submarines.

MAPPING THE SEABED

Today, sonar helps ships 'see' the seabed, even though it lies far below them in total darkness. They use it to study rock formations, and also to spot shipwrecks or sunken planes. This ship is using multibeam sonar, which sends out a fan-shaped signal. Echoes from the signal describe the shape of the sea floor.

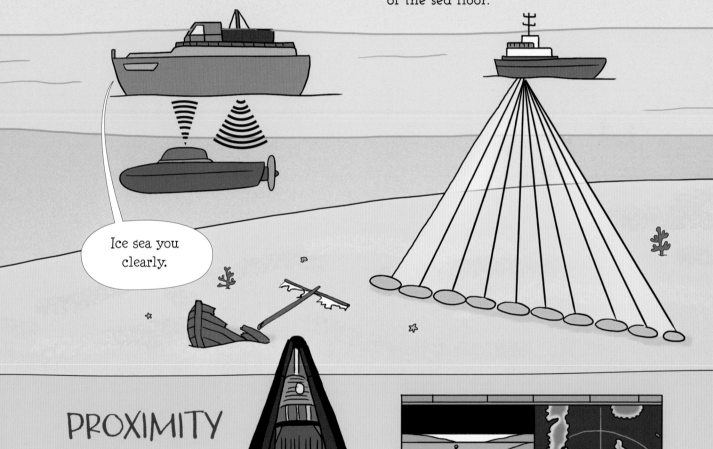

Ice sea you clearly.

PROXIMITY FUSE

Another wartime secret weapon used by the Allies was the proximity fuse. It was a kind of radar fitted into the tip of a shell fired from a gun. Radiation waves detected a target (such as a plane in the air), which made the shell explode.

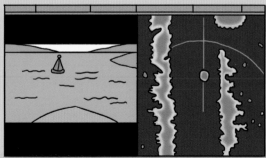

NAVIGATION AID

Today, radar is widely used for peaceful purposes, such as guiding ships at night. A ship's microwave radar scanner sends out radio waves and picks up reflections from solid structures, which show up on screen.

LASER LIGHT

If you've made it this far in the book, you're doing well. Let's face it, light is complicated stuff. And now we get to the really tricky subject: lasers! We use lasers every day – in CD and DVD players, for instance, and laser printers and laser displays. So who invented them, and how do they work?

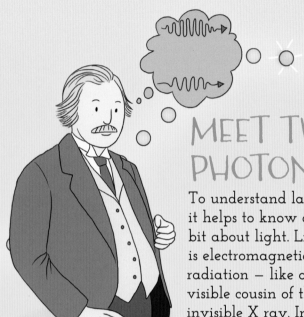

MEET THE PHOTONS

To understand lasers, it helps to know a bit about light. Light is electromagnetic radiation — like a visible cousin of the invisible X ray. In 1905, German scientist Albert Einstein described light as made up of tiny bits called photons, often shown as squiggles: wave-packets.

HOW A LASER WORKS

At the centre of a laser is a cylinder filled with a gain medium: a gas or crystal. At each end of the cylinder is a mirror; one with a small hole. The gain medium is 'pumped' with electricity or with light energy (photons). The photons excite the gain medium, which gives out more photons. Eventually, the photons fire out from the end of the laser.

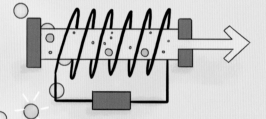

LASER BUILDERS

The first working laser was built in 1960 by Theodore Maiman in the United States. But he couldn't have done it without the pioneering work of other scientists in the US, Russia and Iran in the 1950s. Some of them are shown below.

Charles Townes

Arthur Schawlow

Gordon Gould

Ali Javan

SUPER-CUTTER

Lasers, once described as 'a solution looking for a problem', are used today in all sorts of devices. A cutting laser, for instance, will cut metal, wood and fabric. It can cut anything from very thin, delicate parts up to 12-mm-thick (0.5-in) steel. The cutting pattern is computer-guided.

My lidar is faster than your car...

LIDAR GUN

Police use lidar guns to check on unsafe driving. Lidar works a bit like radar, but uses laser light instead of radio waves. It is super-accurate, homing in on a single car and gauging the speed in a split second. If you see one pointing at your car, tell your parents to slow down...

LASER BROOM

One of the dangers facing astronauts is the growing amount of space junk: bits of old spacecraft orbiting Earth at high speed. One speck of metal hitting your spacecraft could cause a catastrophe! One day, NASA may use 'laser brooms': Earth-based laser weapons that could zap the junk and push it out of harm's way.

LANGUAGE

Language is as old as humanity itself. Writing originally came from art: if you wanted to say 'sun' or 'bear', you drew a picture of the sun or a bear. Gradually, down the years, these drawings became coded letter systems: alphabets. Today, around the world, there are more than 6,000 different languages. But except for the most recent languages, we simply can't say who invented them.

FIRST ALPHABET

People first used alphabets about 5,200 years ago in the Middle East, mainly for writing about taxes and trading. This Sumerian scribe is using a reed to punch wedge shapes in wet clay (which later dried). Sumerian wedge-letter writing is called cuneiform.

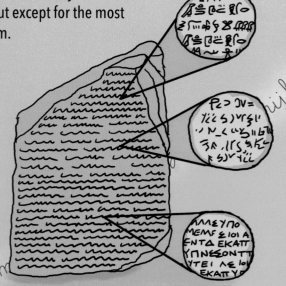

ROSETTA STONE

Ancient Egyptian priests used pictograms we call hieroglyphs ('holy carvings'). For ages, we didn't know what these meant. But in 1799, a French soldier in Egypt discovered an old stone tablet carrying the same message in three languages. At last we could work out what those priests were scribbling.

PICTOGRAMS

The very earliest writers used pictograms — shapes describing things. So, a pictogram for 'water' was often a wavy line, and 'ox' was a horned head. Later, people began using simpler shapes, which were quicker to draw than pictograms. (A bt lk txtn ur frnds.) This table shows some early writing systems from the ancient Middle East.

Original pictogram	Later pictogram	Assyrian cuneiform	Meaning
			Mountains
			Fish
			Ox
			Grain
			To Go

PITMAN SHORTHAND

Fast-forward to 1830s England, where a teacher, Isaac Pitman, believed that people spent too long writing. 'Time saved is life gained,' he said. Too right! Isaac invented a shorthand language of simple lines and squiggles. Each shape stood for a sound or for a simple word (like 'the' or 'you'). Pitman shorthand is still popular, saving people time today.

SIGNALS

Before radio, sailors hung flags, like laundry, on their ships' masts to send signals. Captain Fred Marryat devised a basic flag code in 1817, and 40 years later it grew into the International Code of Signals, with 26 flags. You can send a message with a single flag: the A flag means 'I have a diver down.' Or you can string lots together to make words.

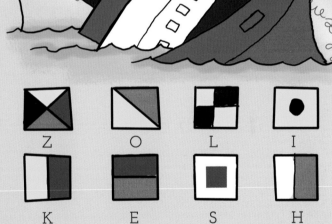

Z   O   L   I

K   E   S   H

ESPERANTO

Esperanto is a language invented in 1887 by Polish doctor Ludwig Zamenhof. He wanted to make it so easy that anyone could use it: a kind of international language. Currently, more than two million people can speak Esperanto.

WRITING IT DOWN

What is written **on** is as important as writing. You can't carry stone tablets to the shops! Early people made writing material from plant fibres, and parchment from animal skins. Paper came much later, and pencils and pens are really very recent.

SYMBOLS

The very earliest writing yet found is a group of symbols found at Jiahu in China. They were carved onto tortoiseshells and bones about 8,500 years ago. No one's quite sure what the symbols mean. Magic spells, perhaps.

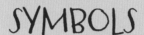

Grandad?

What a pong!

PAPER

The ancient Egyptians mashed strips of papyrus, a marsh plant, into flat sheets for writing on, and so gave us the word 'paper'. Around 105 CE in China, Tsai Lun made wrapping paper from rags, bark and old nets.

INK

For ink, early Chinese used a mixture of boiled animal skin, burnt bones, burnt tar and soot. Phew, stinky!

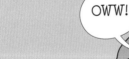

OWW!

TATTOOING

Centuries ago, the Māori of New Zealand made tattoo ink from caterpillars and burnt tree gum, and used sharks' teeth as tattoo tools. When Europeans arrived, Māori began adding gunpowder to their ink.

POST-IT

The great thing about sticky Post-It notes is that they're not too sticky, so you can reuse them lots of times. American Arthur Fry invented the Post-It note in 1974, using a not-too-sticky glue invented a few years earlier by Spencer Silver.

I INVENTED THIS!

GRRR!

Don't even think about it!

STAMPS

The first glue-backed stamp was the British Penny Black of 1840. Rowland Hill, a teacher, introduced it to make letters easier and cheaper to send. To buy an original Penny Black today, you'll need £3-4,000,000 ($3.8-5,000,000)!

BIRO

The ballpoint pen is called the 'biro' after Hungarian László Biró, its inventor in the 1930s. Or was he? In fact it was American John Loud's idea, in 1888. He used his ballpoint for writing on leather (when no longer on the cow), but he never benefited from his invention.

Better than wearing an ear tag!

MINE

MINE

MINE

PENCILS

The first pencils were simple sticks of graphite dug from mines in the hills of Cumbria, northern England, as much as 500 years ago. Shepherds used them to identify their sheep.

PRINTING

The invention of printing was one of the biggest technological leaps in human history. It meant that if you learned to read, you could learn anything written in books. Like these little facts. So it's slightly surprising that printing took so long – more than 1,000 years – to spread from its birthplace in China to the cities of Europe.

WOOD-BLOCK PRINTING

Chinese Buddhist monks began wood-block printing as early as 200 CE. They carved pictures, such as flowers, and text into wood, then used the carvings to print on silk. (Like a rubber stamp, the uncut parts made inky marks; the cutaway parts did not.)

TYPEWRITER

American William Burt came up with the 'typographer' – possibly the world's first typewriter – in 1829, but it didn't work terribly well. He'd invented it to make secretaries work faster, but it was actually slower than handwriting!

DOH!

TOY PRINTMAKER

This 'John Bull Printing Outfit', made by Carson Baker Ltd of London, was a popular toy in the 1950s. Each letter was on a little rubber block, and you arranged them in slots to form words. Trouble was, they pinged off all over the place, then went into the vacuum cleaner.

MOVABLE TYPE

With movable type, printing became easier. The printer Bi Sheng made Chinese characters from porcelain (baked clay) around 1045. His type enabled thousands of copies to be printed.

The printer coats a metal plate with wax, then arranges porcelain characters on the wax to form words.

He warms the plate to soften the wax, then lays a flat board on the characters and presses them into the wax.

After inking the characters, he lays a sheet of paper over them and presses it to transfer the ink. Then he peels the paper off.

Yay! Only 1,285 pages still to print...

PRINTING PRESS

Printing with movable type became popular in Europe after Johannes Gutenberg introduced it to Germany in the 1440s. He also designed the first printing press. His early work for the church included a bible. It took about half a day to arrange the letters for each bible page — and there were 1,286 pages! All up, it took his workers about three years to print 180 copies. But it was easier than writing the bible out by hand.

SENDING OUT SIGNALS

The next time you text someone, spare a thought for your ancestors from before the computer age. Doing 'chat' involved things like smoke, mirrors, lights, arm signals... But the rise of electric power in the 18th century brought a wave of new inventions based on the telegraph. At last, they could send messages instantly over long distances, simply by pressing keys.

SMOKE SIGNALS

As soon as humans learnt to control fire, they could also control smoke, by placing damp grass on a fire. Ancient Chinese and Greeks, as well as Native Americans, used smoke signals, often to warn of danger.

It says your home is on fire.

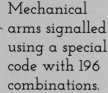

Mechanical arms signalled using a special code with 196 combinations.

SEMAPHORE

Ever waved your arms to attract help? Frenchman Claude Chappe put this old trick to use when he invented a semaphore system in 1792. As each station received a signal, it passed it on to the next. Chappe's network of stations eventually spanned all of France.

Bad signal today...

HELIOGRAPH

A mirror, reflecting sunlight, makes an excellent signalling device. German surveyors used this idea in the 1820s. About 1869, Henry Mance, a British official, invented the Mance heliograph, a sun-signalling instrument with a range of 56 km (35 miles).

FAX MACHINE

Alexander Bain was a canny Scotsman who invented the electric clock and also laid telegraph lines along the Edinburgh–Glasgow railway. In the 1840s, he devised one of the first faxes: machines that 'telephone' exact copies of text and pictures to people. Few people use the fax today, now that we have email.

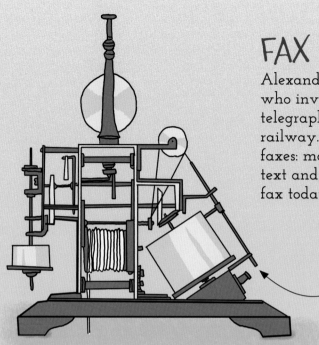

Some of the moving parts for Bain's fax machine came from his clock designs.

TELEGRAPH

The first really practical telegraph was invented in 1837 by William Cooke and Charles Wheatstone, for use on the new railways that were now snaking across Britain. It used five wires, sending signals to five magnetic needles, which pointed to letters. Though easy to use, it was expensive, so they came up with a single-wire telegraph in 1845.

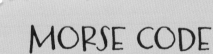

Letter

Needle

Electrical connectors

'Dit... dit... dit-dit-dit... dah... this is driving me dotty.'

MORSE CODE

Morse code is named after American Samuel Morse, but others — Joseph Henry and Alfred Vail — helped with his 1836 invention. You used the electrical tapper to send a code of short signals (dots, or 'dits') and long (dashes, or 'dahs'), and the person at the other end decoded it to read the message.

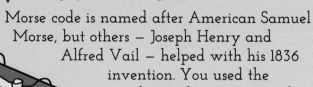

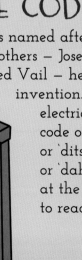

RADIO

Radio, TV, computer, mobile phone, walkie-talkie – all these communication tools use radio waves. These are rather like light waves but are invisible, though just as fast. Once radio waves were understood, the race was on to invent new ways of communicating.

Electricity plus magnetism make...

RADIO WAVES

The discovery of radio waves began with Scotsman James Clerk Maxwell (left). In 1864, he suggested that magnetism and electricity working together could create invisible waves.

One full 'wave' (from one crest to the next) is called a cycle. The length of one cycle is the wavelength.

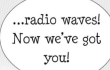

...radio waves! Now we've got you!

In 1885, German scientist Heinrich Hertz (right) tested Maxwell's theory, using a spark gap as an antenna. When a spark jumped the gap, it showed it had picked up radio waves. The cycle (waves per second) was named a hertz (Hz), in Heinrich's honour.

So who invented radio? We've lined up some suspects...

TESLA

Serbian **Nikola Tesla** worked in the USA for Thomas Edison, then on his own. He invented giant 'Tesla coils' to send and receive radio waves. In 1892, he designed a radio, but his lab burnt down before he could test it. So Marconi is credited as the inventor of radio.

MARCONI

In 1894-97, a young Italian, **Guglielmo Marconi**, used transmitters ('senders') and receivers ('getters') to send radio signals over steadily greater distances. He went to Britain and demonstrated his kit by transmitting across the Bristol Channel. In 1901, he sent a message over the Atlantic.

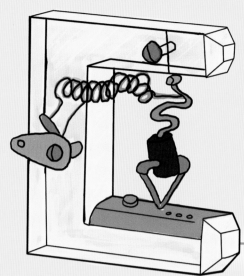

TRANSISTOR

The bulky vacuum tube was replaced in 1947 by the transistor. The first transistor, designed at Bell Labs in the US, looked like a tangle of burnt spaghetti, and it was big! Modern transistors are so tiny you can fit millions into 1 sq in of circuitboard.

The first transistor radios of the 1950s were portable – handy for annoying people.

The vacuum tubes in early radio sets made them very warm!

VACUUM TUBE

The vacuum tube, invented by Englishman John Fleming in 1904, and improved on by American Lee de Forest in 1907, allowed for big changes in current. It was used in radio, TV and, from the 1940s, the first computers.

J C BOSE

Jagadish Chandra Bose of India was an all-round genius who also wrote sci-fi novels. His experiments with new equipment in the 1890s helped other radio pioneers (like Marconi), but he wasn't interested in making a system of communication.

STUBBLEFIELD

Nathan Stubblefield, an American farmer, invented a kind of wireless broadcasting system in the 1880s-90s. In 1902, he demonstrated it by sending a message 'from Santa Claus' to some schoolkids in a field. But it wasn't true radio; it used magnetic induction.

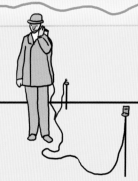

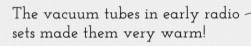

TELEPHONE

Scottish-born Alexander Graham Bell usually gets the credit for inventing the first workable telephone in 1876, but over the next few years nearly 600 people challenged him with inventions of their own. The reason was money: if you could file a patent for one of the world's most useful inventions, you could make a lot of cash! And of course, people have done that, all the way up to Apple with its iPhone. Here are some of the highlights.

THE TRUTH...

Antonio Meucci, an Italian-American, invented a practical telephone before Bell, but his 1871 patent was unclearly worded, and Bell outsmarted him. Although Meucci died penniless in 1889, honour was restored 113 years later, when the US Congress said that Bell had stolen his ideas.

The phone is my invention!

Too bad!

The horse does not eat cucumber salad.

How'd you get my number?

ANOTHER VOICE

Johann Reis, a German schoolteacher, invented a telephone in 1861. It wasn't very good, but it worked, although Reis used an odd message to test it (see left). He even invented the name 'telephon', which means 'far voice'.

CAR PHONE

Early phones were, of course, connected to the wall by electric cable (and many still are). The first mobile phones came much later. This MTA model, made in 1956 by Swedish company Ericcson, was one of the first car phones — but you needed a big car!

SMARTPHONE

The first smartphone? Hmmm, well. The Simon Personal Assistant, launched by IBM in 1994, enabled you to send emails and texts, or check your calendar... but the battery lasted only about an hour!

IPHONE

The iPhone arrived in 2007, and was the brainchild of Steve Jobs (1955–2011), co-founder of Apple. Many Apple workers helped invent it. One was John Casey, who created the 'Telipod', from the iPod and a telephone, in 2000. This became the iPhone.

VIDEOPHONE

In the mid-1960s, the Bell company launched this Picturephone, for making video calls, but it wasn't very successful. Today, we have apps such as Skype, invented in 2003 by Scandinavians Niklas Zennström and Janus Friis.

I can seeeeeee youuu.

MOBILE NETWORKS

Mobile phones use 'mobile networks': ground stations that provide a connection. Some phones connect instead through the communications satellites orbiting Earth. The first satellite phone call was made on 10 July 1962, using the newly launched Telstar 1 satellite.

Early Bird (1965) was one of the first communications satellites (comsats).

MOBILE PHONE

The first practical mobile phone was this Motorola DynaTAC of 1973. Martin Cooper at Motorola famously phoned Joel Engel at Bell Labs to tell him they'd beaten Bell to an invention.

CODE

Lots of communication methods use codes – the semaphore, heliograph and Morse tapper used code to make their flags, flashes and dit-dahs readable. But codes can also provide secrecy. Since ancient times, we've used code to keep messages out of enemy hands, and cracking important codes has helped countries win wars.

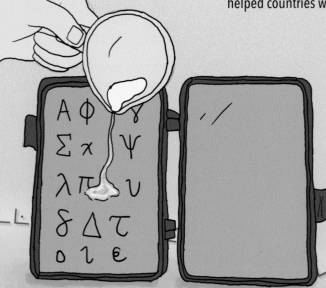

HIDDEN MESSAGE

Demaratus, a Greek living in Persia in 480 BCE, wanted to warn the Greeks that the Persians were building an army. So he took a wax 'notebook', scraped off the wax, and wrote his message on the wood base. Then he rewaxed it. This was smuggled to the Greeks, who scraped off the wax to find the message. Not really code, but still clever.

MESSAGE STICK

The people of Sparta, an ancient Greek city-state, wrote messages on strips of animal hide. They spaced the letters widely. When the recipient wrapped the strip around a wooden pole of the correct size, the letters lined up to reveal the message. You can do this code trick with a strip of paper around a pencil or a broom-handle.

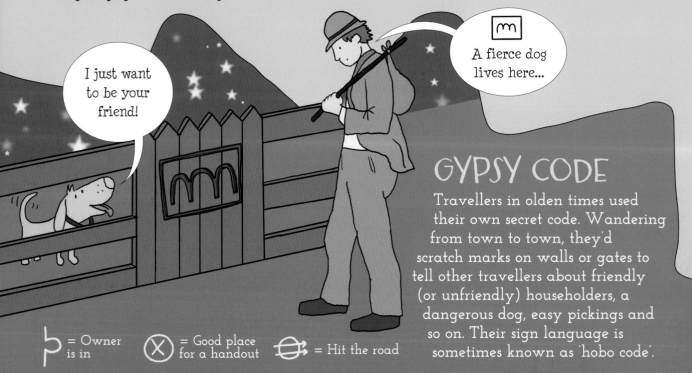

I just want to be your friend!

A fierce dog lives here...

GYPSY CODE

Travellers in olden times used their own secret code. Wandering from town to town, they'd scratch marks on walls or gates to tell other travellers about friendly (or unfriendly) householders, a dangerous dog, easy pickings and so on. Their sign language is sometimes known as 'hobo code'.

= Owner is in   = Good place for a handout   = Hit the road

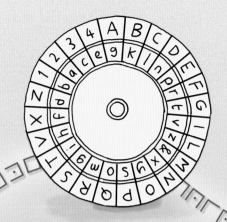

THE GREAT CIPHER

Codes used seriously – in war, for instance – can be very hard to break. In 1626 in France, Antoine Rossignol and his son invented a code in which each French syllable was represented by two or three numbers. Their code was known as 'The Great Cipher'. It was so strong no one cracked it until 1893!

Where are the French hiding?

Um... 34 – 561 – 192, Sir...

CIPHER DISK

This cipher disk was invented by Italian Leone Alberti in the 1460s. It has two discs of different sizes, each with an alphabet, and the two sets of letters can be lined up. The outer ring, or plaintext, is used to set messages into ciphertext (the inner ring). Decoding depends on knowing which two letters to line up.

GUIDANCE SYSTEM

In the US, actress Hedy Lamarr and composer George Antheil invented a guidance system for torpedoes in World War II. It used a piano roll (from self-playing pianos) to create unbreakable codes. It was not used at the time, but later led on to Wi-Fi and Bluetooth.

CRACKING ENIGMA

In World War II, Nazi Germany's secret messages were coded using a machine called Enigma, invented by Arthur Scherbius in 1918. The Poles were the first to crack the Enigma codes, and they taught their methods to the British, French and Americans. This helped the Allies to win the war.

TV AND VIDEO

In TV's early days, to send an image, you had to chop it up into bits, then transmit the bits to a receiver, then rearrange the image from the bits. The first efforts were mechanical – with moving parts – and the picture was fuzzy. It wasn't till better radio technology led to electronic broadcasting that crystal-clear pictures appeared on our screens.

NIPKOW DISK

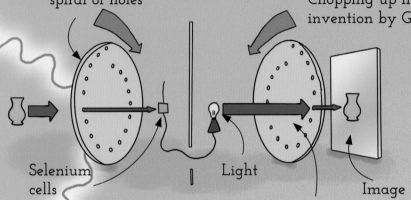

Rotating disc with spiral of holes

Selenium cells

Light

Image

Second disc rotating at the same speed

Chopping up images began with an 1884 invention by German Paul Nipkow. The Nipkow disk was a spinning circle with a spiral of holes. It projected images onto a photo-electric sensor, which turned them into light/dark 'messages'. A second Nipkow disk unscrambled the messages to recreate the image.

JENKINS TV

In America, C. Francis Jenkins designed a Nipkow-style TV in 1923 and launched the US's first TV station in 1928. Francis also invented the waxed paper carton (for juice or milk) and an aircraft catapult.

JOHN LOGIE BAIRD

The father of TV was arguably Scotsman John Logie Baird. He was so poor, he built his early equipment from junk. In 1928 he made the first transatlantic TV broadcast, from London to New York. The next year, he began broadcasting for the new BBC television service.

THIS is entertainment!

Baird's first home-built TV scanner included some Nipkow disks, an old hatbox, darning needles, bike lights and plenty of glue.

CATHODE RAY TUBE

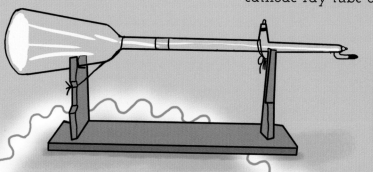

Old TV sets — the fat, heavy ones — contained a cathode ray tube or CRT. Inside this, a beam of electrons shone at a phosphorescent (glowing) surface — the screen — to make the image. German scientist Karl Braun invented the first CRT in 1897, and Russian-born Vladimir Zworykin improved on it in the 1920s (example pictured). With the invention of the CRT, television had become electronic.

FLASH-MATIC

The world's first TV remote control was the Zenith 'Lazy-Bones' of 1950. A wire connected it to the set. Much more space-age was Zenith's 'Flash-Matic' of 1955, which shone a 'magic light' at your TV to change the channel or volume. (Unless of course your dog was sitting in the way.)

Umm, Flash, geddout the way!

VIDEO CASSETTE RECORDER

I can't see a thing, Bing!

Before the invention of the DVD in 1995, the video cassette recorder (VCR) was used to record and play back programmes. American singer Bing Crosby wanted to record his shows, so he helped the Ampex company develop the first VCR, the VR-1000, in the 1950s. It was as big as a gas cooker!

COMPUTERS

The computer is perhaps the single most important invention of our time. The first computers, invented less than a century ago, were like dinosaurs – big body, small brain – but not so today. A single modern smartphone is millions of times more powerful than all of NASA's computers from 1969. (And they managed to put men on the Moon!)

WEAVING ORIGINS

The idea for the computer program came from the French weaving industry over 250 years ago. To weave a pattern on a Jacquard loom, you fitted it with a chain of cards, each punched with a set of holes. The patterns of holes told the machine which threads to pick.

MECHANICAL COMPUTERS

Englishman Charles Babbage (1791–1871) designed the first mechanical computers: the 'Difference' and 'Analytical' engines. They were huge, with thousands of moving parts, for doing tough maths. But he was never able to complete their construction.

COMPUTER WHIZZES

The first computer programmer was Ada Lovelace (below), daughter of famous poet Lord Byron. She worked for Charles Babbage. Grace Hopper (1906-92) a rear-admiral of the US Navy, wrote computer code, including the COBOL language. It's said she also invented the term 'computer bug', when a moth fell into her equipment.

DATA

The US Census Bureau collected information on American citizens, such as birth and marriage dates. To help sort the data, Herman Hollerith, a Bureau worker, invented a series of 'tabulating' machines from the 1890s onwards. These used hole-punched cards to hold the data.

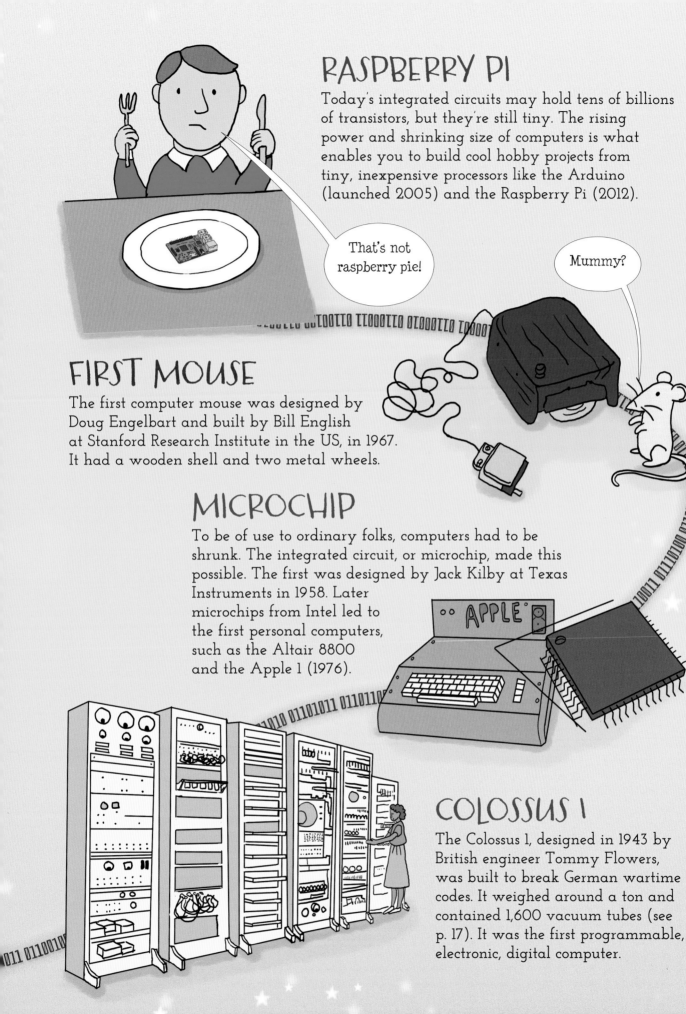

RASPBERRY PI

Today's integrated circuits may hold tens of billions of transistors, but they're still tiny. The rising power and shrinking size of computers is what enables you to build cool hobby projects from tiny, inexpensive processors like the Arduino (launched 2005) and the Raspberry Pi (2012).

FIRST MOUSE

The first computer mouse was designed by Doug Engelbart and built by Bill English at Stanford Research Institute in the US, in 1967. It had a wooden shell and two metal wheels.

MICROCHIP

To be of use to ordinary folks, computers had to be shrunk. The integrated circuit, or microchip, made this possible. The first was designed by Jack Kilby at Texas Instruments in 1958. Later microchips from Intel led to the first personal computers, such as the Altair 8800 and the Apple 1 (1976).

COLOSSUS 1

The Colossus 1, designed in 1943 by British engineer Tommy Flowers, was built to break German wartime codes. It weighed around a ton and contained 1,600 vacuum tubes (see p. 17). It was the first programmable, electronic, digital computer.

THE INTERNET

Just a few decades ago, the Internet was a bit like a club, open only to certain groups, such as scientists and government departments. Today, going online is as easy as picking up the phone. Every day, more than a billion people use Facebook; every minute, over 300 hours of video are uploaded to YouTube. But where did it all begin?

ARPANET

The first version of the Internet was ARPANET. The network was set up in 1969 just for DARPA: the Defense Advanced Research Projects Agency. This US government department of inventors wanted to share ideas between chosen groups. One way of sharing was by email, which was invented @ ARPANET by Ray Tomlinson in 1972.

PACKET-SWITCHING

The Internet communicates by packet-switching. This is a way of sending little electronic 'packets' of data along shared pathways. It was created in the 1960s by Leonard Kleinrock and Paul Baran in the US, and Donald Davies in the UK. In 1973, Vint Cerf and Bob Kahn in the US wrote TCP: the 'rules' for packet-switching. That year, too, ARPANET became 'the Internet', and went international.

WORLD WIDE WEB

The World Wide Web (WWW) is all the information on the Internet. It was created by English computer scientist Tim Berners-Lee. In the 1980s, Tim worked with CERN, a European nuclear research organization. He invented HTML (Hyper Text Markup Language), and CERN began using it, on what was to be the world's first web page.

INSTAGRAM

Kevin Systrom and Mike Krieger invented Instagram, the photo- and video-sharing service, in 2010. Two years later, Facebook bought Instagram for roughly $1 billion.

FACEBOOK

The social networking website, Facebook, was invented by American student Mark Zuckerberg in 2004. He first named it 'Facemash', but luckily he changed his mind. Four years later, he became the world's youngest ever billionaire.

👍 1,000,000,000

RFID

The IoT uses RFID — radio frequency identification. Credit cards, shop security tags and microchips in pets and farm animals all use RFID to connect via electromagnetic fields. Many people helped create RFID. For instance, Russian inventor Léon Theremin used it for a bugging device for spying on the Americans, in 1945.

INTERNET OF THINGS

One day, your family's car, fridge, computers and maybe even your pet will all be hooked up to the Internet. It's called the Internet of Things (IoT), and it's already begun. The first 'thing' on the IoT was a soft-drinks machine at Carnegie Mellon University in the US, in 1982. Students checked online whether it contained chilled drinks, to save checking for real.

AGRICULTURE

Farming today involves high technology, big tractors and complex soil science – but it still relies on the ancient inventions, such as the plough and windmill, with which our ancestors first tamed wild land and made it productive.

SIMPLE PLOUGH

Once we had domesticated cattle, perhaps 8,000 years ago, the ard followed. This simple plough made from wood, and later metal, scratched single furrows in the soil.

HEAVY PLOUGH

On this ninth-century heavy plough, a coulter makes the first cut in the soil. Behind that is the share, which turns the soil, helped by the mouldboard.

SHADUF

Ancient Egyptians used the shaduf to draw water. On the short end, a weight of clay or stone balanced the bucket end, making it easy for one person to lift.

Hey chum, jump on and I'll give you a lift.

What about us?

WHEELBARROW

Who invented the wheelbarrow? No one's quite sure. Possibly it was the ancient Greeks. But certainly the early Chinese were using it by around 200 CE. (It was the Chinese, too, who first domesticated pigs and chickens.)

LIGHTWEIGHT PLOUGH

This plough of 1730, designed in Rotherham, England, by Joseph Foljambe, was simple to build, and its iron-clad mouldboard made a clean cut.

TRACTOR

Today, you can hitch a multi-bladed plough (or any other farming tool) to the back of a tractor. The tool uses power supplied by the tractor's engine..

WINDMILLS

The first windmills were probably invented in eighth-century Persia for grinding grain or drawing water. They worked 'sideways', turning horizontally inside walls that funnelled the wind through the vanes.

ARCHIMEDES SCREW

The Archimedes screw lifts water by turning a spiral. It's named after the Greek genius Archimedes (287-212 BCE), but may have been invented centuries before he was born.

WATERWHEELS

Some 2,000 years ago at Barbegal in France, the Romans built a 'staircase' of 16 connected waterwheels. (The picture shows just the bottom wheel.) They used the mill to grind grain into flour.

FOOD TECHNOLOGY

Your kitchen pantry probably contains cans and jars of preserved food. And you'll have devices to keep food cool (a fridge) or hot (a Thermos flask). But, centuries ago, there were no such conveniences – not even proper cookers. So who invented them all?

FIRST CAN

In 1810, Frenchman Nicolas Appert came up with the first 'can'. He sealed food in a glass jar capped with cork and wax, and boiled it. It would then stay fresh. To prove the method, he once preserved a whole sheep!

Duh, no label – hope it's peas, not dog food.

RING PULL

The ring pull on a drink can was invented in the USA in 1959 by Ermal 'Ernie' Fraze. Within two decades, his company was earning half a billion dollars a year from his clever little tab.

TIN CAN

These are the world's first tin cans, made in London in 1813 by the firm of Donkin, Hall & Gamble. Trouble was, the tin opener wasn't invented till 1855! That's why these men are opening the cans with a hammer and chisel.

THERMOS

Around 1892, Scottish chemist James Dewar invented the vacuum flask, for keeping liquids cool (or hot). Sadly, he didn't patent the idea, but the German company Thermos did... and the rest is history.

FIRST FRIDGE

The first fridge was this ice machine, invented in America by Oliver Evans and built by Jacob Perkins in 1834. It used a terrifically complicated pumping system to remove heat and cool the water.

FRANKLIN STOVE

In 1741, brilliant American Ben Franklin invented a fireplace with openings that let out more heat without lots of smoke. Modestly, he called it the Franklin stove.

COCA-COLA

In 1886 in Atlanta, Georgia, American chemist John 'Doc' Pemberton began selling a fizzy drink as a 'brain tonic', which he described as 'pure joy'. Its name? Coca-Cola.

CHEWING GUM

You could cook on a Franklin stove, too. Here, John B. Curtis is heating a pot of sticky resin from spruce trees in 1848, to make America's first chewing gum.

IRON AND STEAM

With the invention of the steam engine three centuries ago, and with it the ability to make plenty of good iron and steel, the Western world entered an industrial revolution. Steam, on its own or in partnership with electricity, would power the new factories, steamboats and railway locomotives.

PAPIN'S STEAM ENGINE

French-born physicist Denis Papin, helped by Gottfried Leibniz, invented one of the first steam engines in 1707, and planned to fit it to a steamboat. But the boatmen on the river Weser in Germany, afraid of the new technology, stopped him carrying out his plan.

PURE IRON

To build the early steam engines, they needed good, pure iron — lots of it. In 1709, Englishman Abraham Darby I worked out how to purify iron by heating it with coke (coal that has been 'cooked'). Newcomen's pumping engine used iron from Darby's furnaces.

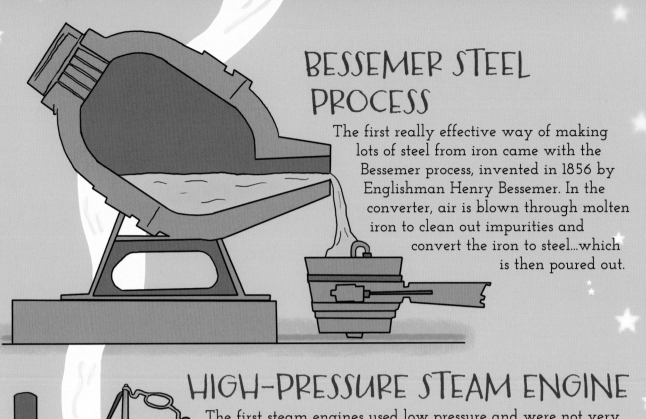

BESSEMER STEEL PROCESS

The first really effective way of making lots of steel from iron came with the Bessemer process, invented in 1856 by Englishman Henry Bessemer. In the converter, air is blown through molten iron to clean out impurities and convert the iron to steel...which is then poured out.

HIGH-PRESSURE STEAM ENGINE

The first steam engines used low pressure and were not very powerful. That changed with the high-pressure steam engine, invented by Englishman Richard Trevithick in the 1790s. It would drive industrial machines, steamboats and the world's first railway locomotive.

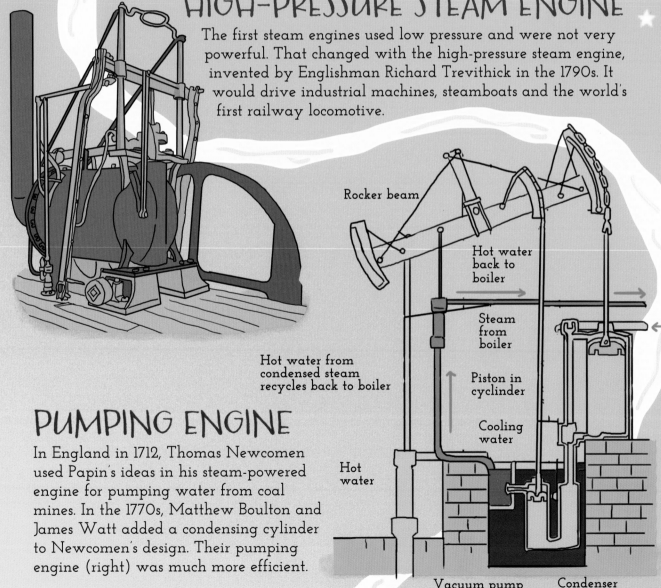

Rocker beam

Hot water back to boiler

Steam from boiler

Hot water from condensed steam recycles back to boiler

Piston in cyclinder

Cooling water

Hot water

PUMPING ENGINE

In England in 1712, Thomas Newcomen used Papin's ideas in his steam-powered engine for pumping water from coal mines. In the 1770s, Matthew Boulton and James Watt added a condensing cylinder to Newcomen's design. Their pumping engine (right) was much more efficient.

Vacuum pump   Condenser

THE TEXTILE REVOLUTION

The steam engines of the industrial revolution, along with water power, drove new machines for making goods, such as woven cloth, in greater quantities than ever before. Society changed dramatically as country folk crowded into towns to work in the new factories.

SPINNING WHEEL

In earlier times, making yarn from wool was slow work. The spinning wheel, invented around 1000 CE in India, sped things up, but spinners still found it hard to supply weavers with enough yarn.

Baaaa!

AMERICAN WEAVING

Industrial weaving came to the US thanks to Francis Lowell, who had secretly copied British loom designs during a visit in 1810-12. He built textile mills in Massachusetts and fitted them with his new, improved looms.

JETHRO TULL

The revolution in mechanized work reached agriculture, too. The English seed drill, invented in 1701 by Jethro Tull, planted seeds in holes at the right growing depth. (Before, seeds had just been thrown across the soil.)

SPINNING JENNY

In 1764, Englishman James Hargreaves invented the spinning jenny, a machine that could spin several spools of yarn at once. One machine did the job of eight, ten or even 100 spinners.

The machine's name, 'jenny', probably came from 'engine'.

Why do they keep calling me Jenny? I'm Maggie.

WATER FRAME

Richard Arkwright's water frame (1767) was a yarn spinner powered by water flow. In his Nottingham factory, belts, pulleys and shafts connected a water wheel to each floor, driving the frames.

ELECTRICITY

Electricity has a long history. Early peoples knew about electric fish, and lightning, and static electricity (the crackly tingle you make by stroking your cat's fur, for instance). But storing electricity, and using it as a power source, dates from 350 years ago.

LEYDEN JAR

This is a Leyden jar. It's a very crude battery or capacitor, capable of storing electricity, invented around 1745 by Ewald von Kleist in Germany and Pieter van Musschenbroek in Leiden, Holland.

Cork lid

Glass jar

Tin foil inner lining

Tin foil outer lining

Water

Electrode (metal rod and chain)

TESLA COIL

Serbian Nikola Tesla (1856-1943) pioneered radio, neon lights, alternating current, X-rays, wi-fi and even a 'death ray' (which luckily he didn't build). His Tesla coil is a kind of transformer.

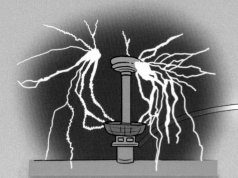

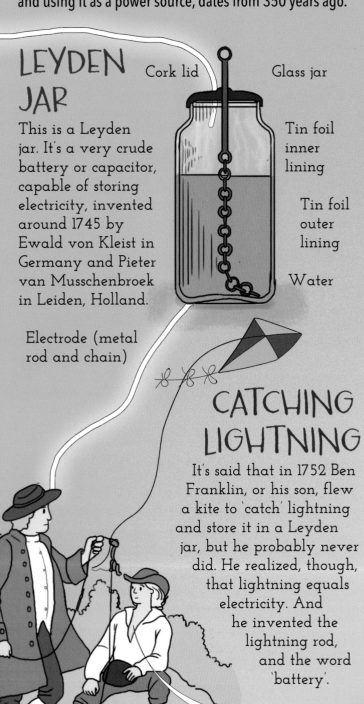

CATCHING LIGHTNING

It's said that in 1752 Ben Franklin, or his son, flew a kite to 'catch' lightning and store it in a Leyden jar, but he probably never did. He realized, though, that lightning equals electricity. And he invented the lightning rod, and the word 'battery'.

Gee Pop, you're a bright spark!

You can wire me to the mains!

VOLTAIC PILE

Italian scientist Alessandro Volta invented his 'voltaic pile', a battery, in the 1790s. His countryman Luigi Galvani had earlier found that if you sent electricity through a dead frog's legs, they twitched — showing that nerve signals are electric 'messages'.

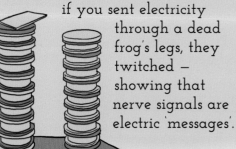

ELECTRIFYING INVENTOR

Frenchman Gustave Trouvé (1839-1902) designed this glowing jewellery. The list of his electrified inventions includes a canoe, outboard motor, dentist's drill (ouch), metal detector, airship, razor, sewing machine, microphone, telegraph, rifle... and more.

My bling may be 'light', but it feels sooo heavy!

LIGHTNING ROD

The 19th century saw a craze for all things electrical. This man has a Franklin rod attached to his umbrella to ward against lightning strikes.

HYDROELECTRIC POWER

The first house ever to run on hydroelectric power (from water flow) was Cragside in England. Its dynamos provided lighting, and powered the nearby farm buildings.

ELECTRIC MOTOR

In 1871, Zénobe Gramme, a Belgian, invented an electric generator or dynamo. It wasn't very good — but he later found (by accident) that his machine, if connected to an electric source, would spin by itself. He had invented the modern electric motor.

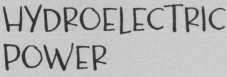

Oops! But then again, hurrah!

FARADAY DISK

English scientist Michael Faraday made the crucial connection between electricity and magnetism. He invented an early electric generator, the Faraday disk, in 1831. It works by spinning a metal flywheel in a magnetic field.

MEASURING TIME

We've come up with all sorts of inventions to measure the passage of time. The ancients saw the sun rise and set each day, and very sensibly used it to measure the hours. Of course, sundials don't work in the dark, so the clockwork mechanism was the next leap forward.

3D SUNDIAL

This 3D sundial, invented in 250 BCE by Greek astronomer Aristarchus, is called a scaphe. The post casts a shadow inside the hemisphere, showing the time. (Aristarchus, by the way, used it to calculate Earth's size, and its distance from the Moon.)

Oh look, it's time for tea!

WATER CLOCK

The ancient Egyptians relied on the water clock, or clepsydra: water dripped from one container into another to measure the hours. (They used it to time people's speeches during debates. No more drip – zip your lip!)

Humph! Tea break is over.

SUPER TIMER

A water clock designed in the third century BCE by Ctesibius of Alexandria is said to have been the most accurate timekeeper of the next 1,800 years.

Mechanical bird (makes chirping sound)

ELEPHANT CLOCK

In 1206, the Muslim engineer Al Jazari invented this water-powered 'elephant clock', which made a sound every half-hour. It borrowed technologies from many ancient cultures, including Indian, Persian, Chinese and Greek.

Hidden water mechanism

Chinese dragon (tips when a ball is dropped into its mouth)

Driver (hits a drum every half-hour)

Time for a nap, I reckon!

Elephant statue

PENDULUM CLOCK

This pendulum clock designed in the 1650s by Dutch astronomer Christiaan Huygens was more accurate than any clock made over the next two and a half centuries. (A pendulum is a weight on an arm, which swings regularly to keep time.)

TICK TOCK TICK TOCK TICK TOCK TICK TOCK TICK TOCK TICK TOCK TICK

WHAT'S THE WEATHER?

Vacuum

Mercury

Glass column

Level of mercury rises or falls with changing air pressure

One way of forecasting the weather is to measure atmospheric pressure using a barometer. This early barometer of 1643 was the invention of Italian Evangelista Torricelli. It reads the changing height of a column of mercury, a liquid metal.

AT HOME

Take a look around your home and school. Some of the basic materials – glass, concrete, brick – date back to ancient civilizations, and it's hard to say exactly who invented them. But all those nifty devices, such as locks, doorbells, elevators and toilets, come from someone's brainwave.

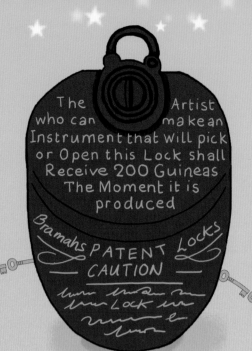

The   Artist who can   make an Instrument that will pick or Open this Lock shall Receive 200 Guineas The Moment it is produced

Bramahs PATENT Locks
— CAUTION —

PIN LOCK

Over 2,000 years ago, the Mesopotamians used key-operated door locks, made from timber. This is an ancient Egyptian pin lock.

CHALLENGE LOCK

High-security locks date from 1784, when British engineer Joseph Bramah designed his 'Challenge' lock. He promised a big cash prize to the first person to pick it (unlock it without a key). It remained unpicked for 67 years! By then, of course, old Joe had died.

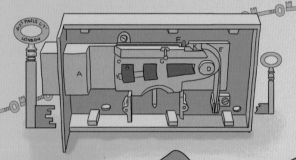

CHUBB LOCK

English locksmith Jeremiah Chubb invented this 'detector lock' in 1818. If you used the wrong key in it, the lock jammed and could only be opened with a special extra key (shown on the right).

ELECTRIC DOORBELL

In 1831, American scientist Joseph Henry invented a doorbell that rang inside a building via an electric wire. Yep: we have him to thank for all those kids who ring the bell and run away. (The electric relay in Joe's bell was later used by Samuel Morse in the Morse code tapper.)

I could get tired of this.

Gotta keep it moving...

TOILETS

If there's one home invention we use every day, it's the loo. It's an old one, too. The Romans had toilets with drains to flush away the poo, and they wiped their bums with a sponge on a stick.

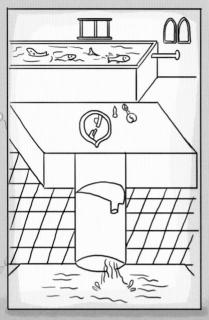

FLUSHING TOILETS

In 1596, English writer Sir John Harington drew this design for the 'Ajax', the world's first true flushing loo. (In his day it was called 'the jakes'.) He probably didn't really keep fish in the water tank, though!

BUILT TO LAST

Locksmith Joseph Bramah also designed flushing toilets. Some of those he built in his London workshop are still working today.

Now all we need is elevator music.

SAFETY LIFT

Early elevators were dangerous: if their lifting cable broke, they could hurtle to the ground, killing the passengers. So, American Elisha Otis invented a safety lift with an emergency brake, and demonstrated it at New York's World Fair in 1854. The cable was cut, and Elisha fell just a few inches in his lift before the brake stopped it. Success!

MATERIALS

Perhaps you've never heard of materials science, but it's big business. Inventors are constantly at work improving the stuff things are made of – making it cheaper, better at its job, better for the environment and so on. Welcome to the history and science of 'stuff'!

MACKINTOSH

The 'Mackintosh' raincoat was invented by Scotsman Charles Macintosh in the 1820s. He made the waterproof fabric by sandwiching rubber between two layers of cloth.

I'm quite dry (so no drippy jokes please!).

VELCRO

Velcro was invented by a dog. Nearly. George de Mestral was walking in Switzerland in 1941, and noticed how the hooked spines of plant burrs stuck to his dog's fur. That gave him the idea for a clingy strip-fastener with one side of 'fur' and another of tiny hooks. Velcro was launched in 1955.

Yup, I invented this!

DUPONT INVENTIONS

Workers at the American company DuPont have a knack of inventing new materials: here's a roundup of some of their most famous.

NYLON

Wartime parachutes were made from nylon, which was invented in 1935 by Wallace Carothers for use in ladies' stockings.

FREON

For years, Freon was the gas used in aerosol cans, and a coolant in fridges. DuPont didn't actually invent it, but starting selling it in 1930. Today, Freon isn't used much, as it contributes to climate change.

TEFLON

Teflon is the non-stick pan coating that helps your parents flip omelettes. Easier to say than polytetrafluoroethylene, it was discovered in 1938 by Roy Plunkett.

GORE-TEX

In 1969, Bob Gore stretched a piece of Teflon to 10 times its normal length... and found that it turned into a new fabric that was waterproof, yet breathable. We know it as Gore-Tex, and it's used in raincoats and walking boots.

KEVLAR

This police dog wears bullet-proof armour made from Kevlar, a super-tough material invented by chemist Stephanie Kwolek in 1964.

MEDICINE

No book, however big, could be big enough to cover all the fascinating stories of medical discovery and invention. So here are just a few medical milestones – from studying the human body, to pain relief, the prevention of disease and simple good hygiene.

STUDYING ANATOMY

Dutchman Andries van Wesel (1514-64), better known as Vesalius, was one of the first scientists to dissect (cut open) dead bodies to see how they worked. He published books full of anatomical drawings.

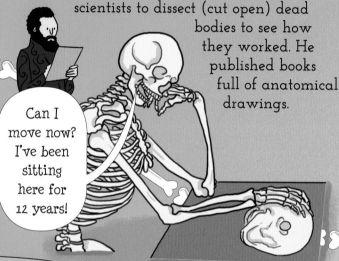

Can I move now? I've been sitting here for 12 years!

FIRST VACCINE

In 1796, English scientist Edward Jenner injected a boy with cowpox, collected in pus from a milkmaid's blisters. It protected the boy against smallpox, which was a killer disease. Thanks to Jenner's pioneering vaccination work, smallpox is no more.

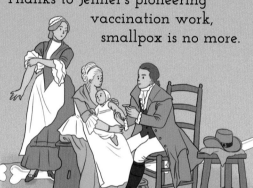

STETHOSCOPE

French doctor René Laennec invented the stethoscope in 1816, when trying to listen to a woman's heart. He rolled up some paper into a tube, put his ear to one end, and heard it clearly. Next, he made a wooden tube. Today's stethoscopes look quite different, but they work the same way.

FALSE TEETH

False teeth were invented centuries ago, possibly in Italy, but some of the most famous were those of US president George Washington (1732-99). They included teeth from hippos, cows, other people, and maybe also elephants!

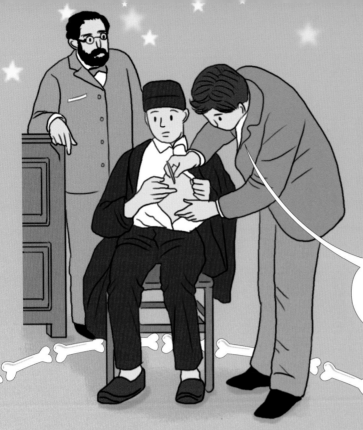

LOUIS PASTEUR

The study of germs, disease and vaccines by French chemist Louis Pasteur has saved countless lives. In 1862, he invented (and gave his name to) pasteurization: heating milk and beer to kill germs. Here, Pasteur looks on as his colleague, Emile Roux, vaccinates a boy against rabies.

Say aaarggh!

The soap's in here somewhere...

HOSPITAL HYGIENE

It's hard to believe now, but surgeons used not to wash their hands before performing operations. In 1847, Hungarian doctor Ignaz Semmelweis believed such uncleanliness was somehow spreading germs and killing patients, and he recommended hand-washing. In doing so, he more or less 'invented' hospital hygiene.

ANTISEPTIC SURGERY

From 1867, inspired by Pasteur and Semmelweis, British surgeon Joseph Lister 'cleaned up' operations by spraying his patients with carbolic acid, an 'antiseptic' or disinfectant. It killed germs and prevented infection setting in.

FACTORIES

It's one thing to invent better products; it's quite another to invent better ways of *making* them. The mass-production factory has a long history, but these days we're realizing that big factories can cause waste and pollution. So we're beginning to make smarter.

Unloading and storage

Sampling

Cleaning

Slicing

Dry screen and mix

Wash and screen

Topsoil

Stones

I've lost the instruction manual.

MASS PRODUCTION

The ancient Phoenicians were early users of mass production. Their ships were assembled from pre-formed parts, almost like IKEA bookshelves or model kits.

ASSEMBLY LINE

Around 900 years ago, the Venetians were also mass-producing ships. They invented the assembly line, where a product passes from one factory area to another as it's built. American carmaker Henry Ford took up the idea in 1913 to assemble his Model T in huge numbers.

ROBOTS

Modern car factories use computer-programmed robots for jobs that are too dreary, dirty, difficult or dangerous for human workers. The first industrial robot was this 1950s Unimate arm, designed in America by George Devol.

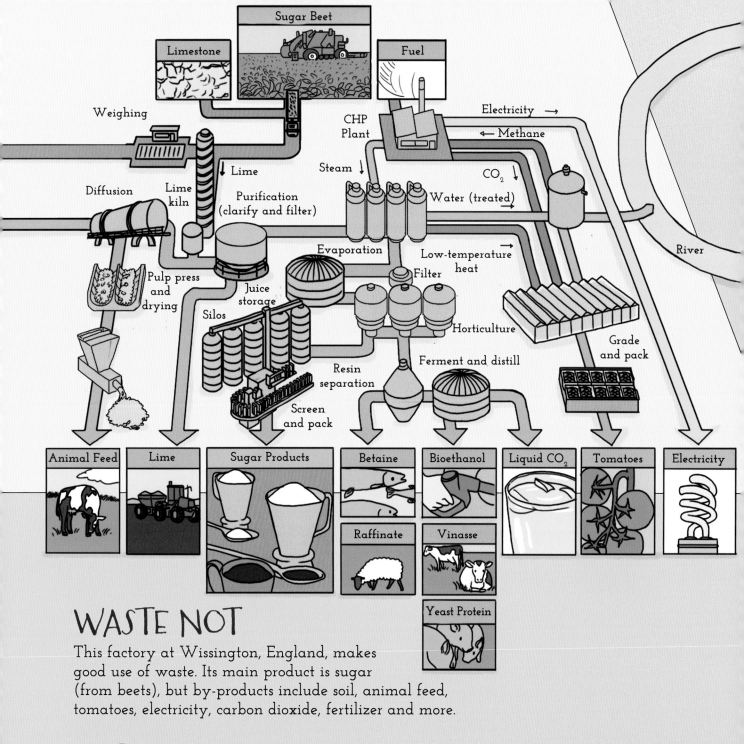

Sugar Beet

Limestone

Fuel

Weighing

CHP Plant

Electricity →

← Methane

Lime ↓

Steam ↓

CO_2 ↓

Diffusion

Lime kiln

Purification (clarify and filter)

Water (treated) →

Evaporation

Low-temperature heat

River

Filter →

Pulp press and drying

Juice storage

Silos

Horticulture

Resin separation

Ferment and distill

Grade and pack

Screen and pack

Animal Feed	Lime	Sugar Products	Betaine	Bioethanol	Liquid CO_2	Tomatoes	Electricity
			Raffinate	Vinasse			
				Yeast Protein			

WASTE NOT

This factory at Wissington, England, makes good use of waste. Its main product is sugar (from beets), but by-products include soil, animal feed, tomatoes, electricity, carbon dioxide, fertilizer and more.

3D PRINTERS

Today, many factories include 3D printers. You scan an object (or design it in 3D modelling software), then turn the object file into a language understood by the printer, which then prints the object.

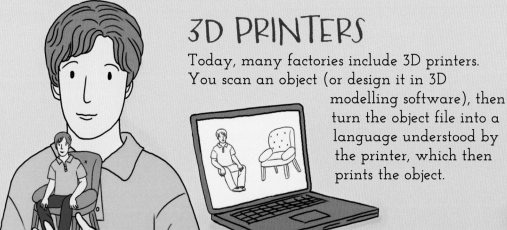

WACKY INVENTIONS

The brilliant English scientist Stephen Hawking once said, 'Mankind's greatest achievements have come about by talking, and its greatest failures by not talking.' So true – but talking isn't always easy. Just look at some of these crazy communication inventions.

It's great-uncle Bill.

DIAL-A-GHOST

It is reported that, in 1920, Thomas Edison, one of America's most famous inventors, proposed making a 'spirit telephone' for talking to ghosts. This story is quite probably made up – but it's a good one.

BAIRD IDEAS...

John Logie Baird came up with good inventions – like TV and thermal socks – but some bad ones too. For example:

• Glass razorblades. His idea was to make a razor that wouldn't go rusty. Trouble was, it just shattered. Ouch!

• Artificial diamonds. Diamonds are a form of carbon. Graphite (pencil 'lead') is also a form of carbon. Diamonds are made naturally underground, by high pressure and temperature. Baird figured he could make them by heating graphite. But all he made was trouble when his experiment cut the power to the city of Glasgow, leaving everyone in the dark.

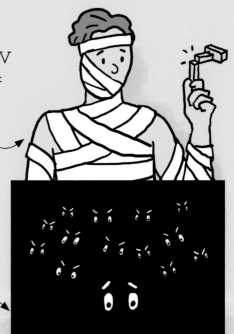

What happened to the lights!?

HOT TENNIS BALLS

American inventor Marvin Middlemark made millions from his Rabbit Ears TV antenna of 1953. He was less successful with a water-powered potato peeler and a plan to rejuvenate tennis balls by microwaving them.

BOW-LINGUAL

Want to chat to your dog? In 2002, a Japanese team invented a machine that listens to your dog's barking, and translates it into an emotion (such as happy or sad), which is shown on a screen. Different versions have been made for different doggy dialects around the world.

PAWSENSE

You know when the cat walks across the keyboard, turning your homework into gobbledy-gook? This piece of computer software could save you. Whenever it detects cat-like typing, it sounds an alarm (which annoys the cat and drives it away) and 'locks down' the keyboard.

CAMPILLO LOONYGRAPH

Some early versions of the telegraph — and there were many of them — were a bit crazy. In 1795, Spanish scientist Francisco Salva Campillo suggested connecting a group of people to electric wires. Each person stood for a different letter or number. Messages coming down the wires would shock each person, who would cry out their letter, spelling out the message. Eek!

INDEX

The Author

British-born Matt Turner graduated from Loughborough College of Art in the 1980s, since which he has worked as a picture researcher, editor and writer. He has authored books on diverse topics including natural history, earth sciences and railways, as well as hundreds of articles for encyclopedias and partworks, covering everything from elephants to abstract art. He and his family currently live near Auckland, Aotearoa/New Zealand, where he volunteers for the local Coastguard unit and dabbles in art and craft.

The Illustrator

Sarah Conner lives in the lovely English countryside, in a cute cottage with her dogs and a cat. She spends her days sketching and doodling the world around her. She has always been inspired by nature and it influences much of her work. Sarah formerly used pens and paint for her illustration, but in recent years has transferred her styles to the computer as it better suits today's industry. However, she still likes to get her watercolours out from time to time, and paint the flowers in her garden!